Alexandre Lebreton

FREEMASONRY & SCHIZOPHRENIA

Understanding the mysteries of power

ⒸMNIA VERITAS.

Alexandre Lebreton

Alexandre Lebreton is a French activist in the "anti-pedocriminality" sphere, i.e. the fight against network paedophilia. Lebreton is an autodidact who works more specifically on "paedo-satanism", sectarian groups practising traumatic ritual abuse and trauma-based mind control.

FREEMASONRY & SCHIZOPHRENIA
Understanding the mysteries of power

FRANC-MAÇONNERIE & SCHIZOPHRÉNIE
Comprendre les arcanes du pouvoir

Translated and published by

Omnia Veritas Limited

⊘MNIA VERITAS.

www.omnia-veritas.com

© Omnia Veritas Ltd - Alexandre Lebreton – 2025

"The 18th century was not only the century of the Enlightenment, it was also the century of secret societies, and most of the contributions to research into the Mysteries came from Freemasons. They saw in the Egyptian Mysteries a model of how an enlightened elite, protected by secrecy, could serve and transmit a truth that was inconceivable or dangerous for the common people."

Jan Assmann - Auditorium du Louvre (07/05/2009)

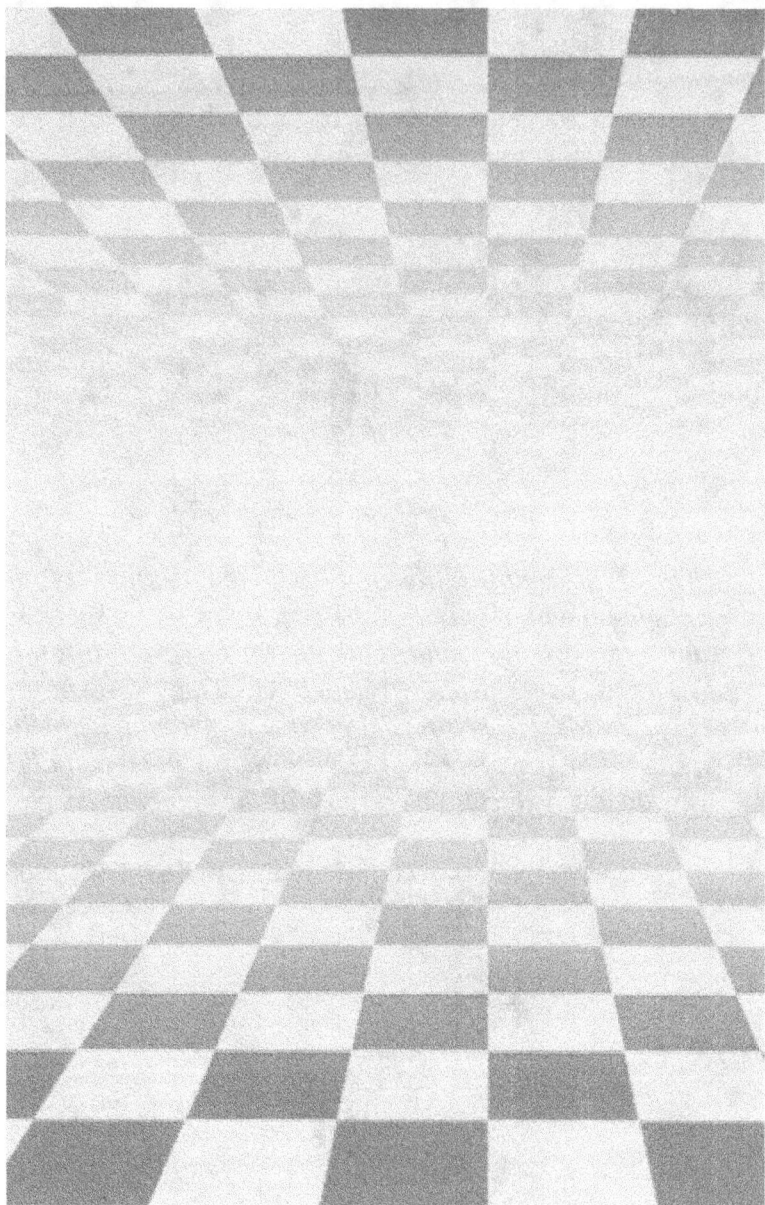

Introduction and disclaimer

This document contains serious allegations concerning Freemasons, which remain presumptions based on testimonies that have not been the subject of judicial investigations. There is no question here of accusing Freemasonry as a whole of perpetrating sadistic and violent rituals; it is probable that some Masons operate without the consent of the majority of lodge members. **The cult of secrecy on which Freemasonry is based poses a problem, even a danger to itself, as it is impossible for it to certify that this kind of "paedo-satanic" ritual practice does not exist in certain back Lodges.** The strict compartmentalisation of this pyramidal hierarchy means that initiates progress "blindly" through this vast sect and its various offshoots. Some of the testimonies contained in this document are particularly difficult and may offend the most sensitive. There is no question here of unhealthy voyeurism, but of exposing criminal acts which, because they have not been brought to the light of Justice, are perpetuated again and again in the shadows.

Readers are advised to disregard preconceived ideas about negative criticism of Freemasonry. Indeed, disapproval of Freemasonry is generally considered to be *anti-Masonry*, akin to *the extreme right*, or even Nazism... However, any bona fide, non-lodge-affiliated individual (whether politicised or totally apolitical) who seriously studies the Masonic question, going beyond the sanitised mainstream press, inevitably comes to question the legitimacy of these occult groups. In particular, their strong presence within public institutions such as the judiciary and the forces of law and order can create a form of *conflict of interest* when a judge or police officer who has taken the Masonic oath puts it before the dignified and loyal oath of his profession... To the advantage of his lodge *brothers* and to the detriment of the layman.

We're going to take a look at the "dual" aspect of Freemasonry, an invisible fraternity interwoven with the visible *humanist* lodge that serves as its showcase: the two are interdependent. But also to the distant origins of this secret society, going back to the Mystery religions and pagan practices. The study of its roots in ancient paganism will lead us down the path of what is known as 'paedo-satanism', which seems to be considered by certain occult groups as a form of initiation for the very young. We will then review a number of testimonies concerning what can be likened to *Masonic ritual abuse* leading to dissociative states or *dual personalities*: the key to trauma-based mind control. Finally, we will see how Freemasonry is itself very interested in 'schizophrenia'...

For a more in-depth study and understanding of these dark mysteries, please refer to the 700-page book *MK Ultra - Ritual Abuse and Mind Control: Tools of domination for the nameless religion.*[1]

[1] *MK Ultra - Ritual Abuse and Mind Control: Tools of domination for the nameless religion*, Omnia Veritas Ltd, www.omnia-veritas.com.

Duality in Freemasonry

The word schizophrenia comes from the Greek *schizein* (to split) and *phrên* (mind), and literally translates as "*split mind*", the fragmentation of the mind, duality. A number of things link Freemasonry to schizophrenia and the notion of duality, starting with the strong symbol of the lodges: the mosaic paving stone in black and white tiles, on which the initiates take an oath: the clash of opposites, the multiple and the One, good and evil interpenetrated and inseparable...

Freemasonry is twofold, it has two natures in one. Freemasons themselves say that everything they do in the lodge has a double meaning. The rituals have a meaning other than that which they would have in the profane world (the world of the uninitiated). The "Venerable Master" strikes a mallet at the beginning of a lodge outfit and declares: "*We are no longer in the profane world*", implying that we are now in a sacred world. In this way, the "Venerable Master" thinks he is sanctifying space and time. In the lodge, the deeper meaning of actions and words is hidden, everything is different, everything is split up and words no longer have the same meaning, even ages, times and dates are different. Newly initiated individuals cannot perceive and understand the profound nature of the cult to which they have already sworn oath and allegiance...

Concerning this Masonic secret (a veritable millefeuille) contained in a double symbolic language that the young initiated "brother" cannot understand, the famous Mason Albert Pike writes in "Morals and Dogma":

"Like all religions, all mysteries, hermeticism and alchemy, Freemasonry reveals its secrets to no-one but Adepts, Wise Men and the Elect. **It uses false explanations to interpret its symbols, to mislead those who deserve to be misled, to hide from them the Truth, which it calls the Light, and thus to keep them away from it. Freemasonry jealously hides its secrets, and intentionally misleads its pretentious interpreters".** (*"Morals and Dogmas", Volume 1, Albert Pike, p.104)*

Let's look at the dual aspect of the Masonic sect, and as we shall see later, a schizophrenic aspect a la **Dr. Jekyll and Mr. Hyde**...

The renowned Freemason Albert Mackey has argued that modern Freemasonry is the result of a fusion between a *"corrupt and black"* form of Masonry practising **traumatic initiation rituals derived from ancient pagan practices**; and a *"pure"* form that involved belief in one God and the immortality of the soul. **He argues that this gives this secret institution both a luminous and a dark side. He defines this dark side, this *'parasitic'* form of Masonry, as a kind of black Masonry with terrifying and traumatic initiation practices, which uses the symbolic representation of the mythical descent into Hades, the tomb or hell, only to return to the light of day: the initiation rebirth - the near-death experience with an astral exit being the ultimate initiation ritual: the resurrection.** (*"The Symbolism of Freemasonry: Illustrating and Explaining its Science and Philosophy, its Legends, Myths and Symbols"* - Mackey, Albert G, 1955)

In Freemasonry, there are two sides, one of which is unaware of the other's existence, which can be translated as *the good guys don't know the bad guys, but the bad guys know the good guys*. This pattern can be found in an internal system of dissociative identity disorder[2] where the 'bad' alter personality (Mr. Hyde) is

---

[2] http://mk-polis2.eklablog.com/le-trouble-dissociatif-de-l-identite-tdi-trouble-de-la-personnalite-mu-p634661

perfectly aware of the existence of the 'good' alter personality (Dr. Jekyll) while the latter is unaware of the existence of the 'good' alter personality (Mr. Hyde). The 'nice' alter personality is the public, visible and benevolent façade, the illuminated tip of an iceberg containing a whole hidden, invisible inner world... This pattern can be transposed to Freemasonry and its very particular hierarchical and selective organisation, where paradoxically, the summit - of the pyramid - *enlightened* or *illuminated*, is the most occult and invisible aspect, to which access is restricted to a minority (*Illuminati* High Masonry).

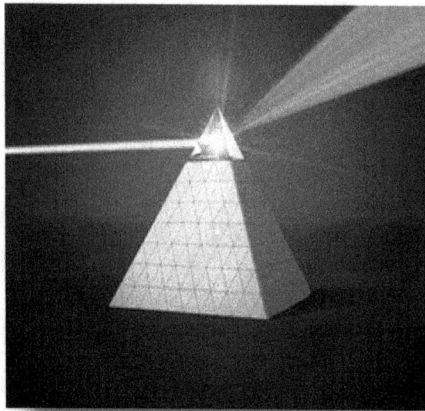

Freemason Manly P. Hall clearly described these two very distinct aspects of the Masonic organisation: *"**Freemasonry is a fraternity hidden within another fraternity:** a visible organisation hiding an invisible fraternity of the chosen... It is necessary to establish the existence of these two separate yet interdependent orders, one visible, the other invisible. The visible organisation is a splendid camaraderie made up of "free and equal men" who devote themselves to ethical, educational, fraternal, patriotic and humanitarian projects. The invisible organisation is a secret fraternity, most august, majestic in dignity and grandeur, whose members are consecrated to the service of a mysterious 'Arcanum arcandrum', that is to say, a hidden mystery."* ("Lectures on Ancient Philosophy", Manly P. Hall, p.433)

Freemasonry is not a "monobloc" secret society, but a superposition of secret societies interlocking with one another. It is a sort of pyramid-shaped *Russian doll of* initiation, where various mystery schools overlap, some opening the doors to others in a highly selective initiation process... Former Freemason Olivier Roney, author of the book *"Gustave Flaubert et le Grand-Orient de France"*, cites, for example, the Gnostic church within the Grand Orient de France, Martinist movements and alchemical schools, etc., all of which are part of the Grand Orient de France. It is well known that these Masonic groups actively practise the most advanced occultism, while the lodges of the first grades are totally unaware of the existence of these esoteric schools: everything is ultra-partitioned and ultra-selective.

A Mason, candidate ready for initiation to the First Degree, prepared ready in a consecrated kerchief beside on his way to the gallows.

Freemasonry never ceases to proclaim publicly that it is not secret, but *"discreet"*, through incessant communication campaigns aimed at lay people. The aim is to soften public opinion so as to dispel the notion that secrecy is synonymous with obscurity and could damage the image of the lodges... and yet... **Secrecy** is indeed at the heart of the Masonic system: proof of this is the fact that the initiate of the first grades has absolutely no idea what the higher grades have in store for him in terms of initiation rituals; he is progressing blindly on his Masonic ascent towards *enlightenment*, as it is strictly forbidden for Freemasons to reveal anything about the higher grades to an initiate of the lower grades. The simple fact that there are *"Small Mysteries"* accessible to the first three grades (blue lodges) and *"Great Mysteries"* reserved for the higher grades, according to the Egyptologist FM Johann Christoph Assmann, proves that this initiatory sect is clearly a *SECRET* society and not the *DISCREET* one they would have us believe... even if they multiply the "open days" for laymen **who are then shown the material decor of the temple... The other side of the spiritual décor will always remain strictly Secret**.

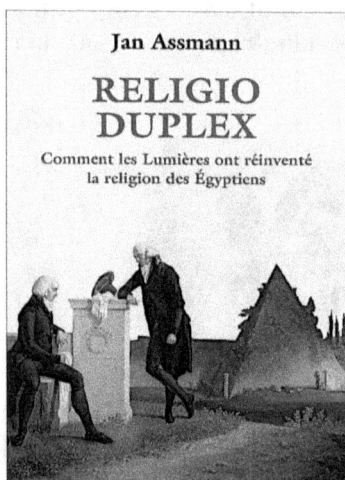

Jan Assmann

RELIGIO DUPLEX

Comment les Lumières ont réinventé la religion des Égyptiens

Assmann, who studied the ancient cults known as *Mystery* Cults, particularly the Egyptians, speaks of a ***Religio Duplex*** (double religion). **He confirms this notion of duality and secrecy by describing a religion with two faces: the exoteric face intended for the uninitiated mass (the showcase) and the esoteric face (the Mysteries) intended for the elite, i.e. a hidden spirituality to be practised and transmitted secretly**. This form of "dual religion" applies the notions of double language or double meaning to signs and symbols, deceiving the layman who is not capable of accessing the Great Mysteries. This is what Albert Pike refers to when he writes: *"It uses false explanations to interpret its symbols, to mislead those who* *deserve to be misled, to hide the Truth from them"*. These "double-bottomed" cults preserve a Gnosis that is only accessible to the *Elect...* This is the hidden fraternity described above by Manly P. Hall and his *"Arcanum arcandrum"*.

This means that the hidden *"Mysteries"* cannot be immediately revealed to young initiates, who would then run away from the sect and its doctrines. For example, **Phallism** or **the cult of the phallus**, , described in detail by the Freemason Jacques-Antoine Dulaure and to which we will return later, is not immediately acceptable to the average person who has just been inducted into a lodge. These Mysteries are infused little by little into the soul of the pretender to *enlightenment*, a Masonic infusion gradually sorting out the souls capable of accessing (and assuming) the Luciferian reality of their lodges. Readers who might be shocked by the association of the lodge with Luciferism will find that the file in their hands gradually supports this assertion...

To quote the high Masonic initiate Manly Palmer Hall: "*When a Mason learns that the meaning of the warrior on the board actually represents a dynamo releasing living power, he then discovers the mystery of his noble profession. Lucifer's seething energies are in his hands. Before he can begin to advance and ascend, he must prove that he is capable of using these energies correctly (...) Man is a god in the making, and just as in the mystical myths of Egypt with the potter's wheel, he must be shaped"*. ("The Lost Keys To Freemasonry" - Manly P. Hall, 1976, p.48)

The horned idol of Baphomet so dear to Satanists

Former Freemason Serge Abad-Gallardo, author of the book "*Je servais Lucifer sans le savoir*" *(I served Lucifer without knowing it)* has stated that *most Freemasons join Freemasonry of course not to worship Lucifer... although at the 29th degree* *there is worship of Baphomet, or more exactly **genuflection before Baphomet**.* (Radio Notre Dame - 01/03/2019)

We should also note the great spiritual schizophrenia of Freemasonry. It is an extremely paradoxical situation in which, on the one hand, it advocates secularism and even atheism and materialism in the secular world, and on the other hand, behind the scenes, it practices the most advanced occultism... Freemasonry publicly declares that "all religion is alienating", but it itself functions with rites, rituals, ceremonies and a shared belief in the GADLU (Great Architect of the Universe). It has its 'followers'... isn't it a religion? **It is the religion of the republic, in the words of the Freemason Oswald Wirth...**

Cecilia Gatto Trocchi, professor of anthropology at the Faculty of Political Science at the University of Perugia and an initiate of a Masonic lodge, said on Italian television: *"When I studied esotericism and occultism, Satanism, black masses, etc., I said to myself that there was something enormous there... **I discovered that it is in fact a long stream of people who have moved from Marxism to esotericism, from a positivist and materialistic vision of life, to a spiritualist and energetic vision. They did this by seeking to invoke the forces of evil in order to gain greater power, knowledge and influence over the world (...) There was a transfer from materialistic secularism to an esoteric and gnostic world that gave rise to occultism. The Pact with the***

Devil is present in deviant Freemasonry, which exonerates Satan. In the lodge to which I belonged, , a mixed lodge, there was the poem "Hymn to Satan" by Carducci. These people think that Satan/Lucifer has done mankind a great favour by giving them the fruit of knowledge, in other words, that the Devil is thus cleared and considered to be a great ally of mankind". (*Enigma*, Rai 3 - 27/02/2004)

As noted above, Albert Mackey states that Freemasonry has both a luminous and a dark aspect. **One of its roots is in Gnosticism, where we find this notion of "Light" versus "Darkness", an essential part of Gnostic theology.** Some survivors of ritual abuse and mind control report how their abusers have deliberately cultivated this split - or duality - in them, with one part of their personality on the *side of the Light* (by attending Christian masses, for example) while another part of their personality undergoes and participates in unhealthy and traumatic ritual practices on the *side of the Dark* - **Dr Jekyll & Mr** Hyde.

The relativism dear to Freemasons, typically Gnostic, allows them to erase any notion of Good and Evil. **This is the Masonic principle of combination or "synthesis of opposites", whose ultimate symbol is the black and white mosaic paving stone placed at the heart of the lodge and initiation rituals.**

The despicable practices, which we will discuss later in the testimonies, are simply a form of going beyond good and evil, giving these *initiates* a kind of feeling of superiority over the masses. The violent and sometimes murderous rituals and extreme sexual debauchery of these sects are linked to notions of transgression, excess of all kinds and violation of social morality. These rituals are seen as the ultimate means of surpassing the human condition and the social order to achieve a kind of human transcendence, all the more so when accompanied by altered states of consciousness due to drugs and dissociative states.

Philanthropy VS Psychopathy?

We note that Freemasonry has a side that can be described as "luminous", the side that it likes to highlight in the public and secular domain: its great *"Humanism"* and its very generous *"Fraternity"*.

In fact, philanthropy (cultural, scientific and humanitarian) is one of the great pillars of the Masonic sect, which is Freemasonry in all its finery, while paradoxically there is a plethora of nefarious, even criminal, dealings among Freemasons...

High Masonic circles are fundamentally dualistic. These individuals strive to balance their evil deeds with good deeds. The greatest philanthropists are often Luciferians of the highest rank, their "generosity" serving their own interests.

In the Anderson Constitutions, one of the founding texts of Freemasonry, there is a complete discrepancy between what it proclaims and what it does. *The search for truth, the study of morality, material and moral improvement, intellectual and social betterment, mutual tolerance, respect for others and for oneself, freedom of conscience,* etc., are the rules that are supposed to reign in the hearts of Freemasons... who are indeed fallible men... But you only have to look at the state of the world today, since humanity has been subjected to this Masonic sophism, to understand the imposture represented by this humanism dripping with good feelings, for so few results... or for so much chaos, shall we say...

Éliphas Lévi had this to say about the Masonic Republican motto: *"Liberté pour les convoitises, Égalité dans la bassesse et Fraternité pour détruire".* (*History of Magic* - 1913, Book V, Chap.VII)

The *Propaganda Due* scandal broke out in Italy in the 1980s. The "P2" Masonic Lodge (Grand Orient d'Italie), led at the time by Licio Gelli, was implicated in a number of criminal cases, including political corruption and the bombing of Bologna station in 1980, as part of a *"strategy of tension"*. This powerful and elitist Masonic lodge, linked to the mafia, was described at the time as *a "state within a state"* or *"shadow government"*. Its members included deputies and senators, industrialists, but also high-ranking military officers, heads of the secret services, magistrates, bankers, heads of the press, etc...

A "State within the State"?! It was under this title that French journalist Sophie Coignard published her book investigating Masonic networks in France. *"It's important to understand that Freemasonry is much more than a social network, it's really a state within the state"*, she said on France 2's TV news programme. She also put her foot down, declaring: *"When a magistrate is a Freemason, when the defendant is a Freemason and his lawyer is a Freemason, and possibly the legal expert too, that can pose a problem!* (Programme *"Revu & Corrigé"*, France 5 - 24/03/2009) Rendering justice involves taking an oath, and when you become a magistrate you take an oath... If you are a Freemason, which of the two oaths takes precedence over the other when it comes to judging? It's obvious that at the level of justice, these Masonic collusions pose a serious problem...

In the case of the Arras insurer (Jacques Heusèle), a highly probable organiser of pink ballets (paedocriminality), the lawyer Bernard Méry stated that a judge clearly told him: "*Maître, there is nothing we can do in this case, you have Freemasonry... What do you want to do against Freemasonry?*" (*Les Faits* - Karl Zéro)... We'll come back to this.

Virtually all of the people indicted in the Lille Carlton partouze affair were Freemasons from the GODF. The facts revealed a system of *aggravated procuring in an organised gang*, as well as *concealment of misappropriation of company assets, fraud* and *breach of trust*. The three judges in charge of the case stated that the affair *was the work of networks of Freemasons, libertines and politicians*. It should be noted that a divisional commissioner, himself a Freemason, used police files to provide information to this network...

In 2013, in Battle Creek, Michigan, the police raided a Masonic temple following a report of several naked people seen behind the windows of the building. The first policeman through the door said he was "*shocked*" by the "*out of control*" situation. He told a journalist present at the scene: "*I saw a couple having violent sex, surrounded by many naked women, there were drugs and men filming the scene.* According to the journalist who spoke to local residents, this was not the first time that an orgy had taken place in this temple... The point here is not to police the "fly police", but to highlight this Masonic tendency towards total disinhibition aimed at overcoming social morality, *taboos* and any notion of right and wrong. As we shall see, these orgiastic activities have their roots in the ancient Mystery cults and rites of sexual magic, notably the Dionysian cult and the Bacchanalia. We shall see that some Freemasons seem to take these deviant practices to extremes, involving non-consenting children and adults in traumatic ritual abuse...

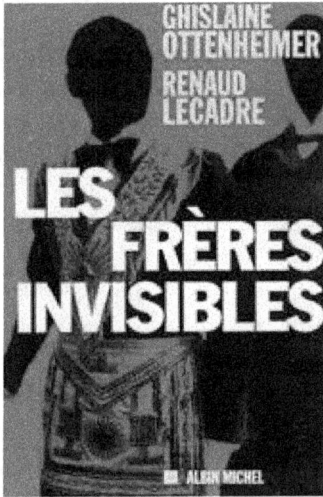

Ghislaine Ottenheimer and Renaud Lecadre, authors of the book *"Les Frères Invisibles"*, report that several Freemasons told them about the *"methods worthy of the worst crime series, used by certain Brothers to compromise their honourable associates"*: **the use of sex clubs with one-way mirrors for taking photos, without forgetting to specify that young children can be used in these "honey traps"**. In this way, everyone holds on to each other's hair. Ottenheimer also explained in L'Express that *some magistrates are afraid of having their proceedings annulled because of Masonic connections* (...) *Masonic justice requires its members to first refer to their hierarchy before taking any action before the courts of the Republic.* **Some have even been expelled for having taken one of their members to civil court without having taken into account the desire of the higher ranks to hush up the matter. How can we believe in the impartiality of this Masonic justice system?**

In Karl Zéro's documentary *"Le fichier de la honte"* (Affaire Zandvoort), we see Juan Miguel Petit, rapporteur for the UN Commission on Human Rights, declare:

*"There have been complaints and specific denunciations from mothers who claim to be pursued by groups, which could be likened to mafias **or lodges, organising child pornography"**.*
Following his investigation in France, Juan Miguel Petit wrote in

his report[3] in 2003: *In several cases communicated to the Special Rapporteur, it was pointed out that the individuals accused of committing (child) abuse were **closely linked to members of the judiciary or to individuals occupying high positions in the public administration, who were in a position to influence the outcome of the proceedings to their detriment**, an argument which had also been put forward by the National Division for the Repression of Offences against Persons and Property...*

Few people know that the man nicknamed *the Ogre of the Ardennes*, the paedophile psychopath Michel Fourniret, was a Freemason. It was journalist Oli Porri-Santoro who revealed in his book *"Le fils de l'ogre"* (The Ogre's Son) that Fourniret belonged to the Grand Orient Freemasonry of France, in the *"Frères Unis Inséparables"* lodge. Oli Porri-Santorro, himself a Freemason at the time, **claims to have received pressure and threats to prevent him from mentioning the link between Fourniret and Freemasonry in his book.** Whether *the Ardennes ogre* was an isolated predator, as he has been portrayed, or whether he was linked to a paedophile criminal network, is another story...

Seeing, for example, members of the Rotary Club (a crypto-Masonic group, founded and made up mainly of Freemasons) selling Christmas tree baubles in a supermarket gallery for the benefit of needy children, or Shriners (a Masonic branch) funding and taking charge of children's hospitals, is *"the light side of the* Brethren*"*; while certain testimonies disturb this peaceful decor by reporting the gang rape of children during

---

[3] http://ekladata.com/619tRjph2N9yyTQQCvlopK-Pac8/rapport-onu-juan-manuel-petit-2003.pdf#viewer.action=download

rituals going as far as blood sacrifice, involving Shriners or Rotarians: *"The dark side of the Brethren"*... - **Dr Jekyll & Mr Hyde** -

For a better understanding of the series of testimonies that will follow, let us now turn to the question of ancient Mystery religions, of which Freemasonry claims to be a continuation. These pagan practices could help us to understand the obscure motivations behind paedo-satanism, traumatic ritual abuse leading to profound dissociative states...

Mystery religions, Paganism and Initiatic Traumatic Rituals

According to the American writer and lecturer Fritz Springmeier[4], one of the secrets of the Mystery religions, in particular the Egyptian cult of the Mysteries of Isis, was the ability to use drugs, torture and hypnosis to create multiple personalities (dissociative identity disorder) in a human being. According to his sources, mind-controlled sex slaves (male or female) are used today in Masonic high degrees and other esoteric back lodges. An alter personality programmed from infancy can serve as a priestess during certain rituals. These slaves, dissociated by trauma, undergo trances, demonic possessions and all sorts of perverse rituals based on sexual magic.[5]

The Mysteries of Isis were essentially based on magic. Egyptian and Isiac sorcery played a considerable role throughout the Old World, and these occult practices have not died out with the modern materialistic world: **they have endured in the teaching of initiatory secret societies of the Masonic type**. *"Ancient magic was the foundation of religion. The faithful who wished to obtain some favour from a god had no chance of succeeding unless they could get their hands on that god, and this could only be achieved by means of a certain number of rites, sacrifices,*

---

[4] http://mk-polis2.eklablog.com/interview-de-fritz-springmeier-p635419

[5] http://mk-polis2.eklablog.com/magie-sexuelle-et-societes-secretes-jean-pascal-ruggiu-golden-dawn-a134245690

prayers, etc...". (M. Maspero, *Études de mythologie et d'archéologie égyptiennes.* Paris, 1893, tome I, p.106)

These cults were particularly prevalent in the Mediterranean basin, including the Babylonian ceremonies of *Inanna* **and** *Tammuz,* the Egyptian Mysteries of *Isis* **and** *Osiris,* the *Orphic* cult, the cult of *Bacchus (*Dionysus*),* the *Eleusis* and *Mithras* Mysteries, the *Corybantic* rituals and the Mysteries *of Attis* and *Adonis.*

Some current testimonies seem to confirm that the cult of Dionysus/Bacchus and all these pagan religions are still practised today in the West. The book *Ritual Abuse and Mind Control: The Manipulation of Attachment Needs* contains the testimony of a survivor of satanic ritual abuse and mind control. The woman was born into a family that practised these rituals from generation to generation. Here is an extract from her testimony: *"The first child murder I can remember consciously was when I was four or five years old* (...) *We were taken to a large stately home, it was during the summer on the occasion of an important date . On the Friday evening there was a ritual followed by a sexual orgy involving many people in costume in this huge salon. Bacchus was one of the gods they worshipped. The next day we went outside to a big meadow, there were about a hundred people there, it was a big ritual. My mother was lying on the ground, in labour. The child was born, a little girl. X then put a knife in my left hand and told me a few things about the child. Then he put his hand over mine and we pointed the*

knife at the baby's chest and killed it. He removed the heart, everyone cheered and went wild, and then the child was dismembered and consumed."

What we have here is a description of a sect that practises sexual depravity and blood sacrifice, which the uninitiated would describe as 'satanic'. This is the cult of Bacchus / Dionysus, whose origins go back to the phallic cult of Osiris (linked to fertility) in ancient Egypt, but whose taste for blood and lust has been multiplied. Immorality, the unheard-of indulgence of the senses and the practice of High Sorcery can be found in most initiatory secret societies. According to the Freemason J-M Ragon, Freemasonry is a *"renovation, a continuation of the Mysteries of Egypt"*, these secret pagan doctrines being renovated into a Gnosis reserved for the "Elect"...

The orgiastic ritual in *Eyes Wide Shut*, or when Stanley Kubrick **brought Bacchus worship to the** screen

The Masonic Order is based on an ancestry containing not only the rituals of the cathedral builders, but also rites from various ancient cults such as the Mystery religions involving, as we shall see, traumatic initiation rituals. In his book *Fils de la Veuve (Son of the Widow)*, Professor Jean-Claude Lozac'hmeur analyses the links between contemporary Gnostic Masonic tradition and mythology. He concludes that the myth of the *Widow's Son,* so dear to Freemasons, contains a veritable parable conveying, in a veiled manner, a secret tradition with which an initiatory cult was originally associated. According to him, once deciphered, this symbolic story reveals a dualist religion opposing an *evil god,* the author of the Flood, to a *good god,* of the Promethean (Luciferian) type. **The *good god* of the various Gnostics would therefore be Lucifer hidden in his most beautiful guise, a 'Liberator God' illuminating the initiates with the light of knowledge...**

In the book *"Le monde grec antique"*, Marie-Claire Amouretti writes about the cult of Bacchus / Dionysus at the Mysteries:

"Dionysus appears as the liberating god, the god of wine and unbridled desire. The whole civic and family framework breaks down during these celebrations, which Euripides evokes extraordinarily well in The Bacchae: Physical intoxication and sexual freedom express a profound need to free oneself from a civic, moral and family system".

Marcel Détienne writes in his book *"Dionysus put to death"*: *"The followers of Dionysus become enslaved and behave like ferocious beasts (...) Dionysism allows us to escape the human condition by escaping into bestiality from below, on the side of the animals.*

In the Dionysian world, practices consisting of group ceremonies **involving blood sacrifices, ecstatic dances and erotic rites** are known as *"orgiasms"*. Dionysus is presented in the dual guise of a god of Nature and a god of orgiastic practices, just like Shiva in India or Osiris in Egypt. **Orgiasm aims to decondition the being, returning for a moment to its deepest, most repressed nature: the door is open to the worst** excesses...

According to the Roman historian Titus Livy, author of *"Rome and the Mediterranean"*, the Romans who investigated the Mystery Cult of Bacchus discovered that **its rituals included sexual transgressions and blood sacrifices.** This is the "**Scandal of the Bacchanals**", a well-referenced historical event.

These various ancient sects seem to have mixed the notion of the fertility of Mother Earth with that of human fertility, bathing in ritual orgies and blood sacrifices linked to a certain calendar to honour and make offerings to the gods and goddesses. The satanic ritual abuses, blood sacrifices and sexual magic that still take place today stem from these ancient Babylonian practices.

In his book *Les Divinités génératrices*, Jacques-Antoine Dulaure (at the time a Freemason of *the Osiris* Lodge *in Sèvres*) confirms that the Mystery cult of Bacchus originated in Egypt and was linked to the phallic cult (the worship of the penis). In his book, Dulaure writes: "*Herodotus and Diodorus of Sicily agree that the cult of Bacchus was introduced into Greece by a man called Melampus, who had been instructed in a large number of ceremonies by the Egyptians. According to Herodotus, Melampus, son of Amythaon, had a great knowledge of the sacred ceremony of the Phallus. It was he who taught the Greeks the name of Bacchus and the ceremonies of his cult, and who introduced among them the procession of the Phallus (...) All that is holiest about these mysteries, what is so carefully hidden, what we are not allowed to know until very late, what the ministers of the cult, called Epoptes, so ardently desire, is the simulacrum of the virile member*".

The Masonic book entitled "*The Master Mason*" (Grand Lodge F.&A.M. of Indiana, Committee on Masonic Education) clearly describes the link between the Mystery cults of antiquity and modern Masonry: "*The idea behind the legend of Hiram is as old as human religious thought. The same elements existed in the story of Osiris, celebrated by the Egyptians in their temples, just as the ancient Persians referred to it with their god Mithras. In Syria, the Dionysian Mysteries contain very similar elements, with the story of Dionysius and Bacchus, a god who died and rose again. There is also the story of Tammuz, which is as old as all the*

*others. **All these stories refer to the ancient Mysteries. They are celebrated by secret societies, just like ours, with allegorical ceremonies during which initiates progress through these ancient societies, passing from one degree to another. Read these ancient stories and marvel at how many men have all received the same great truth, in the same way.***"

In his book *Symbolism of Freemasonry or Mystic Masonry*, 32nd Degree Mason J.D. Buck writes that "***Freemasonry is modelled on the ancient Mysteries, with their symbols and allegories, this is more than coincidental because of the strong similarities***."

In 1896, in *"History of Freemasonry"*, Albert Mackey wrote about the connection between Masonry and Mystery Religions: "*It is well known that in the Mysteries, as in Freemasonry, there are solemn obligations of secrecy with penalties for violation of the oath. I have traced the analogies between the ancient Mysteries and modern Freemasonry (...) **Freemasonry is the unbroken continuity of the ancient Mysteries, the succession of what was transmitted through the initiations of Mithras**"*.

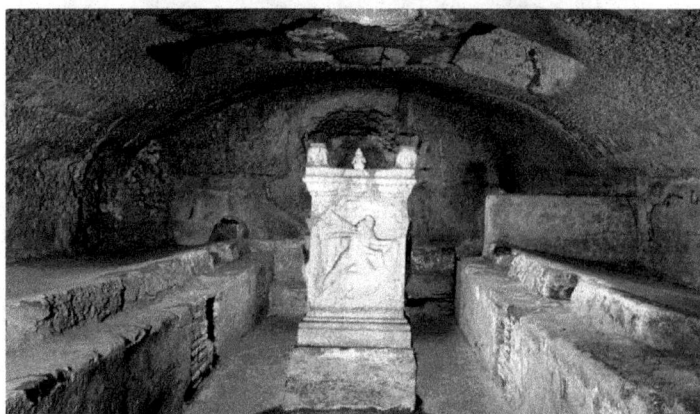

A Mithraic crypt, ancestor of the modern Masonic lodge

The analogies between the Mystery cult of Mithras and contemporary Freemasonry are numerous and undeniable. In his book *Son of the Widow*, Jean-Claude Lozac'hmeur cites several of these similarities. First of all, the Mystery Room of Mithras was underground and included a crypt whose ceiling could be decorated with stars symbolising the universe, just like the ceiling of Masonic temples. The two cults had the same layout: on either side of the hall, lengthways, were benches between which stood four small pillars in the Mithraic temple and three pillars in the Masonic temple. The two columns framing the bas-reliefs of Mithras correspond to the two columns of *Jakin* and *Boaz* in the modern lodges. Last but not least, both cults involve an initiation that is preceded by trials, and they also involve several degrees of initiation. The initiation ritual of the first Masonic degree is virtually identical to the representations of initiation into Mithraism. In both cases, the candidate's eyes are veiled by a blindfold held behind him by a figure, and in both cases the master of the ceremony presents him with a sword. In the Mithras initiation, the candidate is naked and sits with his hands tied behind his back, whereas in the Masonic initiation, the candidate has one arm and one leg naked and stands with his hands free. It is more than likely that we are dealing here with the same cult that has survived the centuries.

Albert Pike himself admitted that Freemasonry was a vestige of the antediluvian religion of the Mysteries, the Babylonian religion: "*The legend of the granite, brass or bronze columns*

*which survived the flood, is supposed to symbolise the Mysteries, **of which Masonry is the legitimate succession** ".* Albert Mackey points out in *"The History of Freemasonry"* that *the traditional history of Freemasonry begins before the Flood. There was a system of religious instruction which, because of its similarity to Freemasonry at the legendary and symbolic levels, has been called by some authors **"Antediluvian Masonry"**.* In his book *"La Symbolique Maçonnique"*, Jules Boucher, also a Freemason, states that *"**present-day Masonry is not a survivor of the Mysteries of Antiquity, but a continuation of the said Mysteries**".*

It is legitimate to ask several questions: does modern Masonry transmit initiations and knowledge similar to those of the ancient Babylonian cults? Has this secret Masonic knowledge retained a doctrine based on paganism, including depraved sexual practices as well as blood sacrifices and baptisms (sexual magic and demonology)? Is this the *parasitic Black* Masonry with its traumatic initiation rituals mentioned by Albert Mackey? This claim by many Freemason writers to be descended from the most shameful "mysteries" of antiquity proves that Freemasonry's doctrines and practices tend towards the restoration of ancient paganism at its most perverse. Sexual magic and the initiatory rituals of Death and Symbolic Rebirth are at the heart of the Mysteries of High Masonry and High Sorcery. **Without knowledge of these occult practices, it is difficult to understand and give credence to accounts of satanic ritual abuse that are beyond the comprehension of the layman.**

In his treatise on sexual magic, Pierre Manoury writes of these rites: "*It should be noted that they constitute ritual practices of energetic manipulation in several traditions; **from certain very closed Western societies, to the sabbats of high sorcery, from Greek bacchanals to priapées and Shiva orgiastic rituals** (...) **certain branches of magic are quite elitist, and sexual magic is one of them**"*.

In the preface to her manual of sexual magic (*The Hanging Mystery*), the Russian occultist Maria de Naglowska clearly sets the tone for these esoteric practices: "*Divinely, the mission of our Triangle consists in straightening out the Evil Spirit in the right way, or, in other words, **in redeeming Satan**.*

One of the 'fathers' of Western sexual magic is Paschal Beverly Randolph. According to him, "*the true power of sex is the power of God*", which can be used both as a mystical experience and for magical practices to obtain money, the return of a loved one or all sorts of other things... Randolph's teachings on sexual magic were widely circulated in many secret Masonic societies and other esoteric fraternities in Europe, particularly the *Ordo Templi Orientis* (O.T.O.). Randolph had founded a religious order dedicated to the *spiritual regeneration of humanity*, called the Brotherhood of Eulis, officially founded in 1874. He claimed that his new sect had its roots in the Eleusinian Mysteries, one of the many ancient Greek religions. Randolph was also linked to the Rosicrucian tradition, but he claimed that the Brotherhood of Eulis was much more connected to the Mysteries than was the Order of Rosicrucians, which he said was merely a gateway to the sanctuary of Eulis: **the deepest secrets of Eulis were largely centred around rituals of sexual magic, linked to the fertility cult of the ancient Mystery religions.** Sarane Alexandrian, author of "*La Magie Sexuelle: Bréviaire des sortilèges*

Pascal Beverly Randolph
MAGIA SEXUALIS
Tehnici sexuale de înlănțuire magică

Sexul este cea mai mare forță magică a Naturii

ANTET

amoureux", reports in her book **that it was the initiatic organisations, i.e. the secret societies, that were responsible for teaching sexual magic to the initiated.** Karl Kellner and Theodor Reuss, two Freemasons of the highest degree, were the founders of the *Ordo Templi Orientis* (O.T.O.), which according to Alexandrian was a veritable school of sexual magic. In 1912, the O.T.O. published in the Oriflamme: *"Our Order has rediscovered the great secret of the Knights Templar, which is the key to all Masonic and Hermetic mysticism, namely the teaching of sexual magic. This teaching explains, without exception, all the secrets of Nature, all the symbolism of Freemasonry and all the workings of religion"*.

Alexandrian asserts that the O.T.O. comprises 12 initiatory degrees and that it is only from the eighth degree that one can begin to approach sexual magic through initiatory masturbation. **The seventh degree focuses on the adoration of the phallus under the symbol of Baphomet.** The ninth degree teaches sexual magic proper, i.e. how to perform the sexual act in order to obtain powers.

The book *Secrets of the German Sex Magicians* gives the three initiatory degrees of sex magic taught by Aleister Crowley and practised by members of the O.T.O. :

VIII° = Teaching of autosexual magical practices (masturbation).
IX° = Teaching of heterosexual magical practices, interaction between sperm and menstrual blood or female secretions.
XI° = Teaching of homosexual magical practices, isolation of the anus (*per vas nefandum*), sodomy, interaction with excrement.

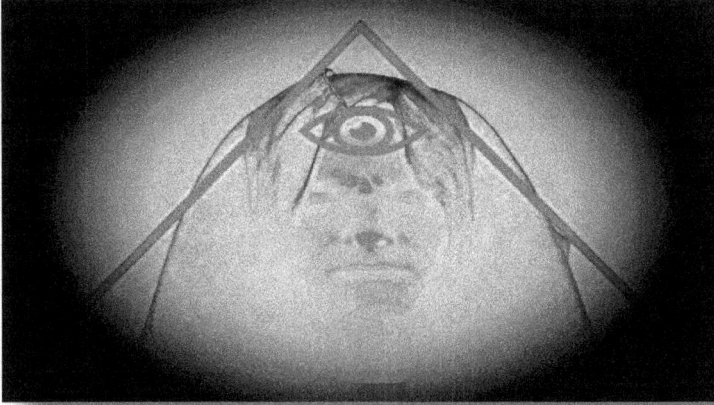

We note that the O.T.O. teachings on sexual magic that come last are those relating to the rectum. In his book "*Shiva et Dionysos: La religion de la Nature et de l'Éros*", Alain Daniélou writes: "*There is a whole ritual linked to anal penetration, to Kundalini (...) this explains a male initiation rite, very widespread among primitive peoples, **in which the adult male initiates have sexual intercourse in the anus with the novices** (...)* This act is also one of the accusations made against **Dionysus organisations.** *This act is also one of the accusations levelled against Dionysian organisations by their detractors, and against certain initiation groups*".

Frater U D∴∴ the author of "*Secrets of the German Sex Magicians*" claims that altered states of consciousness are sought by occultists through sexual rituals to obtain what they call *magical powers*. The author clearly encourages his readers to practise rituals that **overcome sexual taboos** and insists that "***through the use of bizarre and unusual practices, we gain access to altered states of consciousness that provide the key to magical powers***". These are the kind of statements that could explain the accounts of ritual abuse by paedocriminals, whose perversity is beyond comprehension, even going as far as human sacrifice.

Initiatory rebirth rituals involving a symbolic death were widespread in the Mystery religions. These rebirth rites had their roots in ancient fertility cults linked to the Mother Goddess. In the ancient Mysteries, the initiate received the promise of divine omnipotence, a cosmic union with the 'whole', through symbolic union with *the Mother*. In the Eleusinian Mysteries, there was an initiation called the *"Dark Descent"* into the Mother. The hierophant was accompanied in this obscure initiation by a priestess who represented the Mother Goddess, the descent into her womb. In the cult of Mithras, the initiate descends into a pit and the blood of an animal is poured over him. Following this baptism and rebirth, he receives *nourishing milk*.

The famous elitist secret society *Skull and Bones* practices a symbolic death ritual in which the initiate is placed naked in a coffin and must undergo various traumatic stages with the aim of

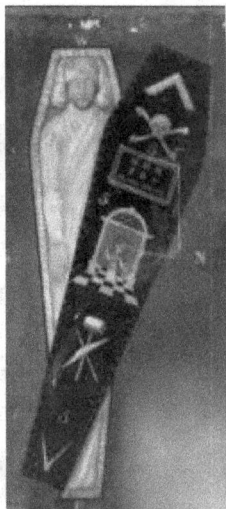

being reborn and transforming his or her life. For *Skull and Bones*, during the night of the ritual the initiate *"dies to the world to be reborn into the Order* (...) *while in the coffin on a symbolic journey through the underworld for rebirth...".* The oath taken by the initiate during this ritual of rebirth swears allegiance to the secret Order that surpasses all that concerns the profane world. In his book *The Satanic Rituals: Companion to The Satanic Bible*, Anton Lavey, founder of the Church of Satan, wrote:

"The rebirth ceremony takes place in a large coffin, in a similar way this symbolism of the coffin is found in most lodge rituals." The most extreme initiatory Renaissance ritual, such as the **"resurrection ceremony"**, consists of inflicting extreme trauma in order to provoke a near-death experience with an astral exit... which can be performed on an adult or... a child. **Learning to suffer, but also learning to cause suffering, seems to be part of the dark initiations**.

The initiation of children through traumatic rituals is not uncommon in paganism. In Druidic initiation, candidates underwent rituals designed to make them transcend pain and fear (confinement in caves, chests or coffins) for several days, only to emerge *born again*. The aim of these initiation practices, known as *mystical fire*, was to achieve a *blaze of light*, in other words a profound state of dissociation. Ross Nichols, a specialist in Druidry and Celtic mythology, writes in '*The Book of Druidry*' that the Druids *immersed or cooked the child*

in mystical fire... **In other words, the child was sometimes subjected to these dissociative initiation tests.**

Let us note here that *the sacred author* of Freemasonry, J-M Ragon, wrote that *"**The Druids of Brittany, who derived their religion from Egypt, celebrated the orgies of Bacchus**".* (F∴ J.M Ragon, Cours philosophique. p. 62) It's a small world...?

Traumatic initiation rituals are designed to transcend consciousness. In her book *A Course of Severe and Arduous Trials*, Lynn Brunet explains that *the trials of the ancient Mystery Cults were designed to produce altered states of consciousness, a mystical experience involving a state of ecstasy and union with the divine. The methods involved exploiting pain, fear, humiliation and exhaustion.*

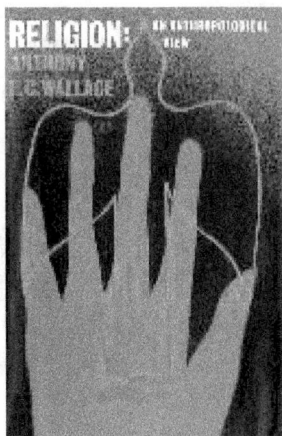

This altered state of consciousness in the face of terror and extreme pain, this *blaze of light* or *illumination*, is what we now call in the light of psychotraumatology: **Dissociation** (see appendix no. 3). This is an essential point to understand when studying paedocriminality and paedo-satanism in particular. Dissociative states, to the point of splitting the personality, are the foundation on which the mental programming - in particular sexual slavery - that certain occultist groups love so much is built...

In his book '*Religion: An Anthropological View*', anthropologist Anthony Wallace describes a **ritual learning process that essentially works with what he calls the '*Law of Dissociation*'. He writes that these practices, which aim to induce an ecstatic spiritual state by directly and crudely manipulating human physiological functioning, are found in all ancient and primitive religious systems.** Wallace classifies these manipulations into four main categories:

- 1) Drugs
- 2) Sensory deprivation and mortification of the flesh through pain
- 3) Sleep deprivation
- 4) Deprivation of food, water or oxygen

Wallace indirectly describes, on an anthropological basis, the origins of Satanic ritual abuse and mind control. He describes how the neophyte is put into a state where he is radically dissociated from all his past knowledge in order to receive new information. Cognitive and affective restructuring (programming) is facilitated in these dissociative states, where the subject's suggestibility is multiplied. Wallace notes that *the effectiveness of these procedures in inducing physiological changes has even been demonstrated in non-religious settings, notably in clinical experiments on the effects of sensory deprivation and various 'brainwashing' or 'thought reform' techniques*. He is referring here to the MK-Ultra programme.

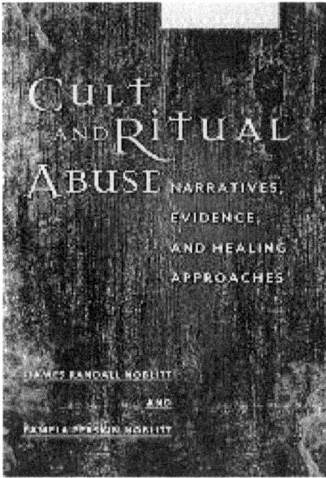

Anthony Wallace speaks of an *ecstatic spiritual state* brought about by certain rituals, an ecstasy provoked by a profound dissociative state. The word *ecstasy*, which comes from the Greek *ekstasis* meaning *exit from the body*, this dissociative *illumination* during trauma is in fact considered by some to be ecstatic, i.e. a state of consciousness where past, present and future are transcended and unified...

Victims of rape, whether adults or children, very often report this phenomenon of extreme dissociation, where **they feel as if they are leaving their physical body at the time of the incident**, observing the scene from the outside, their emotions and physical pain having 'vanished'.

According to the American psychology professor James Randall Noblitt, **trauma has always been seen throughout history as a means of creating altered states of consciousness**: "*There are many ways of creating altered states of consciousness. Obviously you can meditate, do hypnosis, listen to drums and let yourself go a bit... but nothing very impressive will happen... I'm convinced that a very long time ago, some people understood that if you traumatise a person in a certain way, you can create the god you worship* (dissociation with astral exit is an open door to possession by an outside entity). *This is why many ancient religions included trauma in their worship. There is a book on the subject, God is a Trauma, which deals in particular with certain traumatic Gnostic practices dating back to antiquity. We can go back even further, to medieval times, to shamanism and Druidism. This is where mental programming practices began, when individuals noticed that the application of traumatic rituals could produce dissociative states, dissociated identities,* *in other words deities* (possession). *Over time these practices have undergone some changes, but not that many... **You should be familiar with the Mystery Cults that existed in the Mediterranean in ancient times, right up to medieval times. Many of them also involved traumatic rituals. Nowadays, some people claim that the continuation of these cults, namely the fraternal organisations of modern times, the secret societies, also practise this kind of thing.**"*

This extreme form of youth initiation can be found in many cultures. In Papua New Guinea, traumatic rituals designed to terrorise the initiate are an integral part of local cults. Young people undergoing these protocols find themselves totally terrorised by the ceremony, which consists of piercing their nasal septum and burning their forearm. Anthropologist Erik Schwimmer reports that the purpose of the Papuan *Orokaiva* initiation is to provoke *"absolute and lasting terror in the candidate"*. The panic is deliberately induced in the child or adolescent, **who may not even survive the initiation**. Anthropologist Maurice Bloch reports on the effects of the *Embahi* ceremony, which he describes as **symbolically killing the initiate by neutralising his vitality and turning him into a purely transcendental being** (dissociative state). **Following this initiation, the child becomes sacred**...

These are pagan practices that could help us to understand the obscure motivations behind *modern* Satanic ritual abuse aimed at creating the dissociative states necessary for mental control. It's all about sacralising the child through profound dissociative states... An initiatory death with a rebirth to

make the child a killer rather than a victim: a fully-fledged member of the Luciferian cult.

This principle of initiation through trauma is common to all Luciferian/Satanist fraternal structures, **for whom initiation in early childhood is the best way of obtaining a loyal and faithful adult (under mental control), who will perfectly respect the law of silence while perpetuating the obscure tradition of the "Mysteries".** Rituals involving perverse and immoral acts, such as despicable paedocriminality, can also be used to blackmail those involved into silence. This makes it possible to create *"fraternal"* bonds, all the stronger when a human sacrifice, a ritual crime, has been committed in a group and cameras filmed the scene to immortalise it. The followers who immerse themselves in this addictive violence feel connected to each other by a secret that is strictly impossible to reveal to. **It's an unhealthy glue that binds the members together and gives them a feeling of superiority over the profane mass of humanity.** These polytheistic paedo-satanic cults, which practise ritual rape, human sacrifice and blood baptism, worship entities such as Moloch... The repentant Svali (born into a Luciferian cult) reports that the group to which she belonged (San Diego-USA) has practices similar to these ancient Babylonian Mystery religions, including blood baptism: *"The children will take part in rituals during which the adults wear togas, and they must, among other things, prostrate themselves before the guardian deity of their cult. Moloch, Ashtaroth, Baal and Enokkim are all demons commonly worshipped. The child may witness a real or staged sacrifice, serving as an offering to these deities. Animal sacrifices are common. **The child will be forced to take part in the sacrifices and will have to undergo blood***

baptism. They must take the heart or other organs of the sacrificed animal and eat them (...) **They perform initiation rituals with children** *or with older followers,* **the initiate is tied up and an animal is bled to death over him**".

The former Freemason Olivier Roney, quoted above, asserts that the foundations of Freemasonry are based on the cult of Mithras. As we have seen, Professor Lozac'Hmeur has demonstrated the strong similarities between the Mithraic and Masonic initiation rites. Historians report that the Mystery Cult of Mithras performed a blood baptism known as *Taurobole*, a ceremony in which all sins were cleansed with the blood of a sacrificed bull. This was in memory of the divine bull sacrificed by Mithras. Benjamin Walker, author of "*The Woman's Encyclopedia of*

Myths and Secrets", describes this initiation ceremony as follows: "*First there are a few days of abstinence from food and sex, followed by an ablution ceremony after which the candidate's hands are tied behind his back and he lies on the ground as if dead. After certain solemn rites, his right hand is grasped by the hierophant and he is resuscitated. **Next comes the baptism of blood. The initiate finds himself naked in a pit covered by a grating. Above the grating, an animal is sacrificed so that the blood can flow over the candidate. Whatever the animal, it always symbolises the bull of Mithras. The Christian poet Prudentius wrote a description of this ritual, which he remembers personally: "Through the grate flows into the pit the red liquid that the neophyte receives on his body, head, etc.". Symbolically, the initiate has been raised from the dead and cleansed by the revitalising blood of the bull. He is now considered to be 'born again into eternity' and will be welcomed into the community of initiates as a Brother, a Chosen One.*" Regarding this Mithraic cult, it is reported that "*the enigmatic and terrifying initiatory ordeals seem to produce cognitive disorientation in initiated individuals.*" (*Cognitive science, ritual and the Hellenistic mystery religions, Religion & Theology* - Martin Luther, 2006) In Satanic ritual abuse, this cognitive disorientation of the victim is essential to conditioning and mental programming.

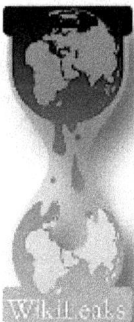 Do certain secret Masonic societies still practise this type of bloody ceremony today... with a potentially traumatic effect? An official document containing the hearings and minutes of **the Dutroux affair in Belgium** (made public by *Wikileaks* in 2009) reports certain testimonies relating to blood sacrifices during rituals sometimes involving a kind of blood baptism. These are statements and complaints, and no proper investigation has been carried out to determine whether the testimonies are true. All these cases are systematically hushed up... Why is that?

Here are some extracts from the document:

- *X1 killed two rabbits and a dwarf goat on B's orders. The orgy took place in the garage. The participants wore special costumes: leather, capes, masks, etc. C. has to eat the heart of the sacrificed rabbit. Children tied to rings in the garage. The blood of the goat was poured over C.* (PV 118.452, 10/12/96, Hearing of witness X1 (Regina Louf), page 542).

- *There were black masses at this address (...) Paragraph 29 (W.'s diary) mentions a family who practise human sacrifices, including their own daughter (...) She was taken to a house where there is a large swimming pool outside. There are lots of men and women. She was made to drink in the car. There's a big fire in the garden. There are three other girls (...) During a game in this house, hot blood was poured over her.* (PV 117.753, 754 and 118.904, Hearing of W., page 749)

- *He attended a black mass in the upmarket suburb of Gent in April 1987. Satanist mass. Animals were sacrificed, disembowelled and then killed. The participants drank the animals' blood (...) T4 was unable to attend the entire ceremony. Description of the villa. Luxurious vehicles (...) J. and E. reported that there were Members of Parliament and other VIPs. Incantations in an unknown language. Priests and priestesses naked under their cloaks. Everyone wearing cloaks and masks. The suffering of sacrificed animals is the means of obtaining power and might.* (PV 118.220, 04/12/96, information T4, page 125)

- *He knows of satanic churches in Hasselt, Brussels, Gent, Knokke, Liège, Charleroi and Mozet (...) The sacrifices range from animal to human. The sacrifices are followed by orgies (...) Sometimes the woman is sacrificed and her blood is used for the rites.* (PV 100.693, 06/01/97, Hearing of L. P., page 126)

- *W. allegedly took part in black masses with other minors. She spoke of minors being branded with red-hot iron and of human sacrifices. She also spoke of prepared human meat that the girls had to eat. During these evenings, the underage girls were raped by the participants. (PV 116.780 21/11/96, Hearing of W., page 746)*

- *In 1985, he took part in several satanic seances near Charleroi. On one occasion, the blood of a 12-year-old girl was offered to the audience. He did not attend the murder (...) on the spot, he was drugged before being taken to a room with masked people dressed in black robes. The participants drank blood. A naked girl was lying on an altar, she was dead* (PV 250 and 466, 08/01/97 and 16/01/97, Hearing of T.J., page 260).

- *She went to the castle for the first time when she was 14 in V. 's beige Jaguar (...) during the full moons (...) She writes: In a circle around the fire - there are candles - everyone stands except the baby and the sheep - the baby cries (...) She describes the killing of the baby and the mixing of its blood with that of the sheep. Then the baby and the sheep are burnt and everyone "makes love together". The baby's heart is ripped out* (PV 150.035, 30/01/97, Hearing of N. W., page 756).

Ritual Abuse and Mind Control in Masonry

Definition

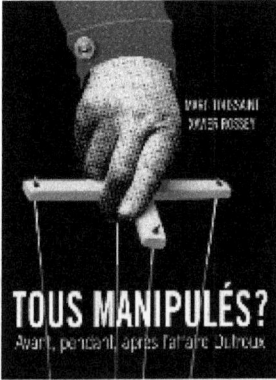

TOUS MANIPULÉS?

Avant, pendant, après l'affaire Dutroux

Despite the detailed evidence of ritual abuse from children, families, adult survivors, police officers, therapists and associations working with victims, despite the remarkable consistency of these reports both nationally and internationally, despite the similarities and overlaps between the various cases and testimonies, society as a whole still resists believing in the harsh reality of ritual abuse. There remains the mistaken belief that criminal "satanic" activities are isolated and rare. This is not a new problem, but society is only just beginning to recognise the seriousness and extent of this phenomenon.

There are many levels of paedophile crime, each more vile than the next...

For some sufferers, it's a matter of satisfying their sexual urges and that's as far as it goes, although they know that these sufferers also operate in networks and may interact with sectarian groups for common interests. For other 'initiated' psychotics, this is part of the occult, i.e. practices that interact with the invisible.

"When you're investigating this kind of case, you also have to look at the hidden side of things, the ritual killings. It's clear that these cases are often discredited and so horrific that people don't want to go any further. For many, these ritual abuses are inconceivable. But once we realise what these acts really involve, we begin to understand that their perpetrators have

separated the notions of good and evil. We know that there are sects and secret societies, that there is an occult power and a cult of power. And there is the belief that good and evil do not exist, that true power lies in overcoming good and evil. These people do not believe in a transcendent force to whom we are accountable. Since there is no value, no God, no responsibility, I do what I want and what I please. I have the power of life and death over whoever I want. That's how these sects are organised. There are two types of paedophile crime: the 'simple' paedophile and the perverse paedophile with a ritualistic side". (Xavier Rossey in Alain Goossens and Hermès Kapf, "*Tous manipulés? Avant, pendant, après l'affaire Dutroux*", Dossiers Secrets d'État, no. 10, August 2010, p. 5).

Former magistrate Martine Bouillon described it in these terms during a famous television debate following an explosive investigation into ritual abuse: "*Child rape - the end of silence*":

- **We've just understood that paedophilia exists, but we can't yet understand that it exists... even worse than 'simple' paedophilia.**

Ritual abuse can be defined as a method of controlling people of any age, consisting of physical, sexual and psychological mistreatment through the use of rituals. It involves repetitive physical, emotional and spiritual assaults, combined with the systematic use of symbols, ceremonies and manipulations for malicious purposes, **usually mind control or mental programming.**

In its National Guide to Child Protection, the Scottish Government's official website provides information on ritual abuse: *Ritual abuse can be defined as sexual, physical and psychological assaults in an organised, systematic way over a long period of time. It involves the use of rituals, with or without particular beliefs. It is usually carried out in groups. Ritual abuse generally begins in early childhood and involves the use of learning and development models designed to reinforce the abuse and silence the victims* (editor's note: mental control). *Some organised groups (networks) use unusual or ritualised behaviour as part of ritual abuse, sometimes associated with particular spiritual beliefs.*

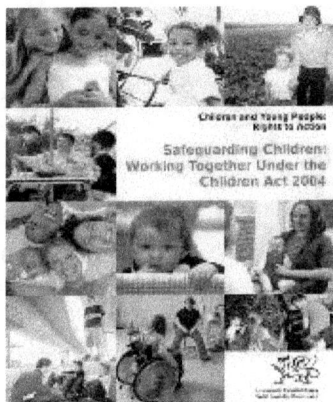

In the UK there is a Department of Health document dedicated to child protection, entitled *Working Together under the Children Act.* In 1991 the document described: "*Organised abuse is an umbrella term for abuse involving a number of perpetrators, a number of children, and generally encompasses different forms of abuse* (...) *Some organised groups may exhibit strange and ritualistic behaviour, sometimes associated with particular 'beliefs'. This can be a powerful mechanism for terrifying abused children so that they do not disclose what they are being subjected to*".

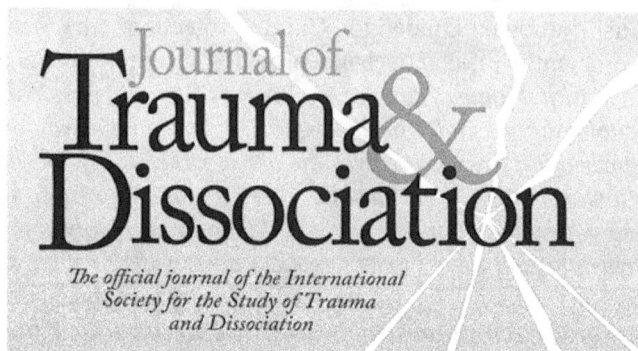

Journal of Trauma & Dissociation

The official journal of the International Society for the Study of Trauma and Dissociation

In 2011, the journal *Trauma & Dissociation* (*International Society for the Study of Trauma and Dissociation*) published a dossier[6] entitled *"Guidelines for the treatment of dissociative identity disorder in adults"*. Here is an extract: "*A substantial minority of patients suffering from Dissociative Identity Disorder (DID) report sadistic abuse, exploitation and coercion at the hands of organised groups. It may be organised around the activities of paedophile rings, child pornography or child prostitution rings, various 'religious' groups or cults, multi-generational family systems and human trafficking and prostitution rings. Organised abuse frequently incorporates activities that are sexually perverse, horrific and sadistic, and may involve coercion of the child as a witness or participant in the abuse of other children. Survivors of organised abuse are among the most traumatised of dissociative patients. Some of these highly traumatised patients have marked amnesia for a large part of their abuse, and the story of the organised abuse only*

ASCA

Advocates for Survivors of Child Abuse

---

[6] https://www.isst-d.org/wp-content/uploads/2019/02/TraitementsAdultesEnFrancais.pdf

emerges in the course of treatment".

In 2006, ASCA (*Advocates for Survivors Child Abuse*), an Australian organisation of lawyers, published a report[7] entitled *Ritual Abuse & Torture in Australia*, from which the following extracts are taken: "*Ritual abuse is a multi-layered crime in which dysfunctional families band together to organise these crimes, exploiting children for profit. The primary exploiter and abuser of the ritually abused child is most often a parent. These groups of abusers are usually made up of two or three families forming a network who offer their own children to be abused by the other members of the network. In his book "Trauma Organised Systems: Physical and Sexual Abuse in Families", Arnon Bentovim describes these families as an "organised trauma system" in which severe trauma defines and shapes the family structure and the interaction between its members. Victims grow up in an environment where violence, sexual abuse and extreme trauma are the norm. In this context of organised sexual exploitation, the violence and incest committed by abusers against their own children can be seen not only as sadistic behaviour, but also as a kind of training in these practices of sexual exploitation.*"

Many victims or perpetrators who have been under the influence of these extremely traumatic practices during childhood and adolescence develop severe dissociative disorders, including multiple personality syndrome (Dissociative Identity Disorder[8]), which is the most extreme level of dissociation psychic. The torturer

---

[7] http://ekladata.com/VDn_XpmtR0tVh9cHq38BrBeTybQ/Ritual-Abuse-and-Tortute-in-Australia-ASCA.pdf

[8] http://mk-polis2.eklablog.com/le-trouble-dissociatif-de-l-identite-tdi-trouble-de-la-personnalite-mu-p634661

may therefore be a second personality (an alter) of the individual, who will not be aware of his *Dr Jekyll & Mr Hyde* functioning because of the amnesic walls that separate the different personalities. He may be perfectly integrated into society and his public persona will give no hint of his occult and violent activities. Ritual abuse aimed at splitting the personality is the cornerstone of mind control, the key to subjugating, exploiting and silencing victims.

Dr. Catherine Gould, internationally renowned for her therapeutic work with child victims of Satanism, declared in 1994 in the documentary "*In Satan's Name*" by Antony Thomas: "*There are certainly bankers, psychologists, people from the media, child protection services and also police officers, **because they have a vested interest in being present in all these socio-professional circles.***

*When I started this work, I thought that the motivations behind paedophilia were limited to sex and money, but I began to realise over the course of my ten years of research that the motivations are much more sinister still: **children are abused for the purpose of indoctrination. Ritual child abuse is a protocol used to mould humans into a cult. It's a matter of formatting children who have been so abused, so subjected to mental control that they become very useful to the cult, at every level... I think the aim of all this is to get as much** control as possible...* "

In her book "*The New Satanists*", Linda Blood (former member of the Temple of Set and former mistress of Lieutenant-Colonel Michael Aquino) reports the testimony of a certain Bill Carmody, who is the pseudonym of a senior intelligence instructor at the FLETC (*Federal Law Enforcement Training Center*): "*Carmody investigated disappearances of children for some time which seemed to be linked to sectarian activities. As a member of a specialist team, he led an investigation into a network operating in several states in the south-west of the United States. Carmody*

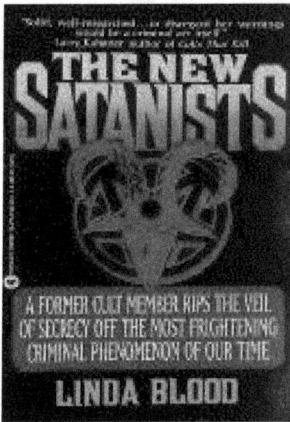

was able to infiltrate a total of three criminal Satanist cults. Commenting on these cults, Carmody said: **"The most serious cults are those that are the most concealed and covered up, in fact these clans have very sophisticated organisations as well as having the best means of communication, it's an international network."**

Bill Carmody claims that these groups traffic in drugs, arms and human beings, as well as child pornography (...) According to him, the best organised criminal cults are run by intelligent, highly educated people from the upper classes of society, where they hold important positions in their communities, so-called respectable positions. These sectarian groups form a highly secretive subculture that is part of the underworld in the broadest sense. They are generally made up of members of trans-generational families whose blood ties help to maintain silence and secrecy.

In 1992, the Utah Attorney General's Office set up a *Ritualistic Abuse Crime Unit* in conjunction with the *Child Abuse Prosecution Assistance Unit*. This government initiative produced a 60-page report [9] entitled *"Ritual Crime in the State of Utah"*, written in 1995 by investigators Matt Jacobson and Michael King for the Attorney General's Office. The

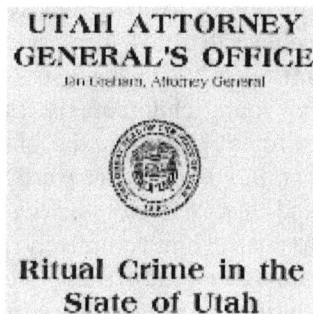

UTAH ATTORNEY
GENERAL'S OFFICE
Jan Graham, Attorney General

Ritual Crime in the State of Utah

---

[9] http://www.saferchildren.net/print/utahag.pdf

report defines ritual crime as follows: "*Ritual abuse is a brutal form of child, adolescent, or adult abuse involving physical, sexual, and psychological violence with the use of rituals. Ritual abuse rarely occurs in isolation; it involves repeated violence over a long period of time. Physical violence is extreme, including torture, sometimes leading to murder. Sexual abuse is painful, sadistic and humiliating. By definition, ritual abuse is not an impulsive crime, but rather one that is maliciously thought out (...) In conclusion, ritual crime cases must be treated like any other case. Investigators are encouraged to keep an open mind when dealing with cases involving the occult, religious beliefs or ritual criminal activity (...) Training and education regarding the many facets of ritual abuse is necessary and should be of great benefit to all levels of the police force. Police officers should be instructed in the basic elements of ritual crime. This training should include the types of organisations involved in occult activities, their aims as well as the symbols used by their members (...) This training should include information on the bizarre nature of ritual abuse as well as the associated problems with multiple personality disorder, amnesia and repressed memories, hypnosis, etc.*".

Testimonials

According to numerous testimonies, there is every reason to believe that this "dark side" of Freemasonry involves "**paedo-satanism**," which consists of practising the worst abominations on young children. The rituals serve as sexual magic for the torturers, who put the child through extreme traumas as *an "initiation"*: in other words, to provoke deep dissociative states and thus "*tear his soul apart*", splitting his personality in order to control him completely. As we have seen, traumatic initiation rituals aimed at creating profound dissociative states are psycho-spiritual practices as old as the hills. These violent cults who

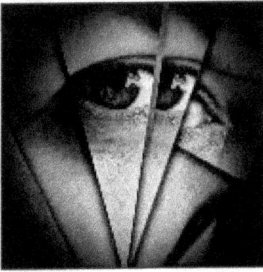

ritually abuse children use various belief system to justify their actions. Some of these beliefs are based on the idea that it is necessary to understand and integrate Good and Evil in order to achieve *spiritual enlightenment*... **This is typically Gnostic, and Masonic Relativism *ultimately* erases any notion of Good and Evil.**

As we have seen, trauma modifies brain chemistry and changes the perception of reality. This is the phenomenon of dissociation, used by certain groups of occultists for a so-called *"Mystical"* experience. **The Luciferians deliberately provoke these sufferings in the child as a process of inversion of sanctification, a counter-initiation aimed at spiritually *unlocking* the little victim: connecting him to other dimensions.**

The 'G' of Gnosis, Darkness VS Light

Many of the participants in these *'modern Bacchanals'* have been immersed in these environments since childhood, and are themselves perverted and programmed from an early age. For them, dissociative states are a veritable addiction and a form of survival in the face of an otherwise insurmountable reality. The problem is that they generally reproduce the traumatic *initiation* practices - in a **Dr Jekyll & Mr Hyde** pattern - on their own descendants...

Caryn Stardancer is a survivor of ritual abuse and mind control, as well as a pioneering activist who co-founded the *Survivorship* group, which she ran for a decade. This support and information group for victims of ritual abuse and therapists is a benchmark in the United States. In 1998, she spoke to Wayne Morris on CKLN.FM radio at Ryerson Polytechnic University in Toronto, Canada:

"I'm a survivor myself, the abuse started in the 1940s, during the Second World War. Some of the things I first saw involved people who worked in the military doing this kind of experimentation. **There were also Masonic connections.** *Around the time I started getting mentoring (within the cult), I was told* **about occult Pantheism** *(polytheism, divination of nature) and exactly what that meant. There are all sorts of systems under which mind control can be exercised. What Pantheistic Occultism*

fundamentally meant was that the belief system doesn't matter, it depends on the adaptability of the individual and how they react to power struggles. **As you progress within the cult according to your ability to adapt, you may never know that there is a larger group, encompassing the one to which you belong** (the ultra-partitioned initiatory Russian doll). *You can access it depending on your ability to evolve within the system, but also through certain relationships with people in that system. For example,* **the people who taught me Pantheistic Occultism were directly involved in what is known as a Dionysian sect.** *It was explained to me that this dated back to pre-Christian times. Essentially, what they were doing was political blackmail.* **The use of children, trained for sex, was aimed at using them to photograph, or film, with adults for the purpose of blackmail** (the *honey traps* dear to the Freemasons). *Ever since I was born into this transgenerational system, there have always been people who spoke of the Occult Tradition, which they traced back directly to* **ancient Dionysism.** *They had a whole occult tradition containing certain historical facts that had come down to their cult.* **This Dionysian sect taught me that one of the earliest laws passed against ritual abuse in Rome, in pre-Christian times, was made against these same Dionysian sects that were still active in the 40s and 50s, and probably still are today! The reason for the laws against them was that at the time it was known that their rituals included sexual orgies, flagellation and ritual rape of women and children. But that's not the main reason why there were laws against these cults, these laws were drafted because these groups practised their crimes for the purposes of political blackmail.**" ("Bacchanal Scandal")

Maude Julien's testimony relates this notion of initiation by traumatising a child to access other dimensions. In her book *"Derrière la grille"*, she describes how her father, **a wealthy entrepreneur initiated into Freemasonry and its secrets**, subjected her to extreme conditioning **aimed at turning her into a** *"Goddess"* **under mental control, a robot obeying his every command**. Maude Julien suffered total social isolation for fifteen years. She was locked in a mental straitjacket, her mind and body trained to make *her a superior being, a Chosen One*. Her father forced her, for example, to hold an electric wire and take electric shocks, a highly effective way of creating deep dissociative states. **The father's aim was to make her capable of** *travelling between universes* **and** *learning to communicate with the dead*... This Freemason initiate obviously knew how the human psyche works in the face of trauma and extreme conditioning, and he set about experimenting this on his daughter...

In a televised interview with Thierry Ardisson in 2014, Maude Julien said: *"My father's aim was indeed to make me a 'super-being', he had a capital mission for me. And to do that, I had*

to undergo physical and psychological training so that the spirit would be stronger than matter."

Maude Julien has confided that she has **traumatic amnesia about scars on her thighs and breasts. She doesn't know what caused it...**

- Thierry Ardisson: *And then there's the cellar... it's quite violent, in other words **he wakes you up in the middle of the night and makes you sit on a chair in a cellar.***

- Maude Julien: *Always to stay put. But the purpose of this capital mission to which he dedicated me was that **I should be able to travel between universes, learn to communicate with the dead...***

- Thierry Ardisson: *There's also the electricity test, which is incredible. **He asks you to hold an electric wire and take electric shocks for ten minutes.***

- Maude Julien: *When there are discharges, you can't react.*

- Thierry Ardisson: *At eight o'clock you go to wake your father, and then you have to hold his chamber pot while he urinates (...) the most disturbing thing is these scars on his thighs and chest, the origin of which you don't know. Do you think these are initiation rites?*

- Maude Julien: **What the doctors are certain of is that they were not done by health professionals, which rules out the accident theory, and I'm afraid I'll never know...**

Is it the occult teachings of the high Masonic lodges that inspire such projects to create *"Higher Beings"*, **enslaved and**

traumatised to become mediums connected to other dimensions? Extreme trauma causes deep dissociative states that spiritually '*unlock*' the child, enabling connection to other dimensions. Are there obscure Masonic rituals whose purpose is to initiate the child, in other words, to create an 'illumination' in the child during dissociation? How far can an initiate go to receive light... or to give it to someone else? To initiate a child, for example? A child who has been tortured and raped during rituals finds himself in a state of profound dissociation, meaning that he himself becomes an open door to other dimensions... In such a state of dissociative trance, could the child be a kind of bridge, a medium acting as an intermediary to link the terrestrial world and the world of spirits, thus serving as a tool for the worst occultists?

Margaret Smith, author of the reference book "*Ritual Abuse: what it is, why it happens and how to help*", herself a survivor of ritual abuse, reports the presence of a certain Gnostic philosophy behind the abuse, as well as the presence of Freemasons, Masonic insignia or Masonic-type ceremonies during traumatic ritual abuse. Margaret Smith publishes some statistics on Freemasonry and ritual abuse in her book:

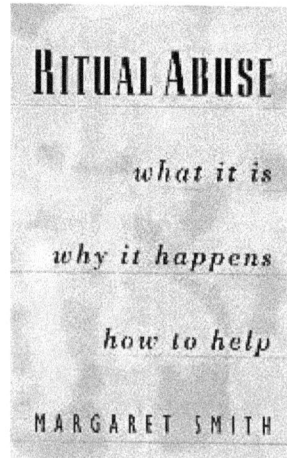

RITUAL ABUSE

what it is

why it happens

how to help

MARGARET SMITH

"In this study, survivors also reported a link between the abuser's membership of a secret

society and the practice of ritual abuse. 67% of survivors said that their abusers were members of secret societies or fraternal organisations. 33% said that family members who abused them were Freemasons". (*Ritual Abuse*, Margaret Smith, 1993 HarperSanFrancisco)

Caren Cook's study *Understanding Ritual Abuse: A study of thirty-three ritual abuse survivors. Treating Abuse Today*, which was conducted on 33 ritual abuse victims from 13 different states, reports that these survivors mentioned two main organisations to which their abusers belonged: Freemasonry (27%) and the Knights of Columbus (9%). Other groups mentioned were the Order of the Eastern Star, the Shriners and the Rosicrucians.

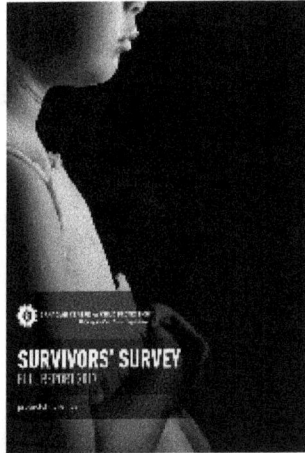

The *Canadian Centre for Child Protection*, a national charity, notes in its 2017 *Survivors Survey Full* Report a series of locations where child abuse takes place. Among the places named by the victims interviewed for this study, it states on page 44: *"at the Masonic lodge to which they all belonged."*

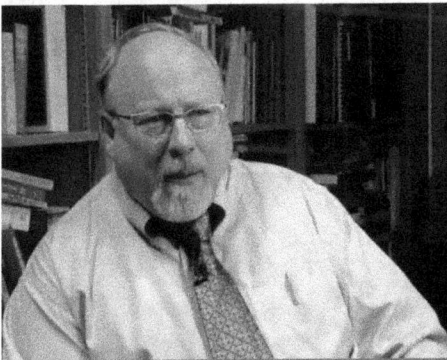

Canadian sociologist **Stephen Kent**, who specialises in deviant religious cults, has met many people who have testified to having suffered ritual abuse of the Masonic type, in particular the children of Freemasons:

"Right from the start of my research, people came forward with testimonies, some of which were linked to Masonic 'abuses'. **Some people claimed that their father had been a Freemason and that the abuse was linked to a lodge and its members. Sometimes, the violence seemed to have taken place within the Masonic lodges themselves.** *These appearances of Freemasonry in a fairly large number of testimonies really left me perplexed (...) Freemasonry does not contain a demonic figure as can be found in Christianity with its rigid notion of God vs Satan. I did, however, find a few mentions of Lucifer, but above all the meaning of certain higher-level rituals, where God appears as a triple character:* **JAHBULON**

"Jah" referring to Jahweh, "Bul" referring to Baal. **Baal is a reference to the ancient pagan gods of the Bible, of the Old Testament, demanding child sacrifices.** *An ordinary Freemason will talk about the god Jahbulon without really being aware of what he's saying* ... **but it's possible that deviant Freemasons, those I call 'ritual junkies', see in this figure a combination of Good and Evil, the combination of a superior god and a god who demands child sacrifices (.... I know that some of the people who made these accusations were talking about Freemasons of the highest degree** (...) *Once I started studying the Masonic question, I discovered that there were people all over North America who claimed to have been ritually abused by Freemasons. A number of organisations based in the United States are particularly insistent that Freemasons practice ritual abuse. In Canada, there is an organisation whose leader is absolutely convinced that she is a survivor of Masonic ritual abuse. So when I discovered that the testimonies I was receiving were part of a much wider North American context, I became much more intrigued by these particularly recurrent accusations* (...) *It's certain 'deviant' groups within Freemasonry that concern me most.* **To me, it's entirely plausible to imagine deviant Freemasons drawing on some of Aleister Crowley's extremist writings, or interpreting to the letter some of his statements about children and sex, or even some of his claims about child or adult sacrifice, and incorporating them into their rituals".** (Interview with Dr. Stephen Kent, Wayne Morris, CKLN-FM - Mind Control Series Part 13)

Stephen Kent also wrote: **"It is worth mentioning that Freemasons are often willing to rent out their lodges to appropriate individuals or organisations, and that few, if any, questions would be asked of a 'Brother' who used the facilities (with a few 'associates') from time to time... Satanic rituals could take place in Masonic Lodges (as some survivors claim in their testimonies) without respectable members knowing anything about it there."** (*Deviant Scripturalism and Ritual Satanic Abuse Part Two : Possible Masonic, Mormon, Magick, and Pagan Influences* - Stephen Kent, 1993)

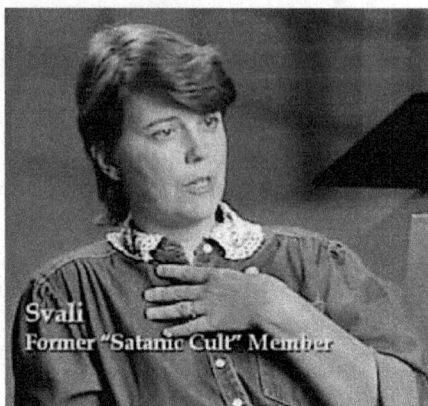

As stated in the introduction to the document, **Freemasonry's strict secrecy and compartmentalisation is a danger to itself**, as it is impossible for it to certify that such occult and criminal practices do not involve some of its members...

American survivor Svali reported: "*For thirteen years, the abuse sometimes took place in a Masonic lodge in Alexandria, Virginia. Some of my abusers were Freemasons, although most of the members of this lodge were unaware that some of them were using it for this purpose.*" (*Cults that abuse* - Svali, 18/04/2000)

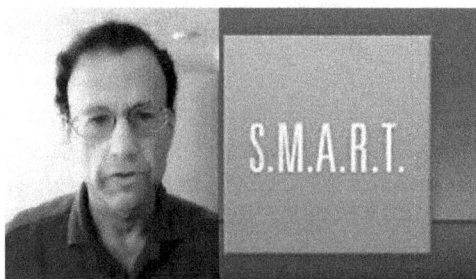

Neil Brick, himself a survivor and founder of the American group S.M.A.R.T. (dedicated to disseminating information about ritual abuse and mind control) said:

"I believe that Freemasonry is one of the largest organisations responsible for satanic ritual abuse in the world. Its connection goes all the way up to government (federal and local), as well as some of the country's economic institutions... I was born into Freemasonry." ("*Surviving Masonic Ritual Abuse*" - Neil Brick, *Beyond Survival* magazine 07/1996)

Here is an extract from Marshall Thomas' book "*Monarch, The New Phoenix Program*", linking Freemasonry to Ritual Abuse/Mind Control:

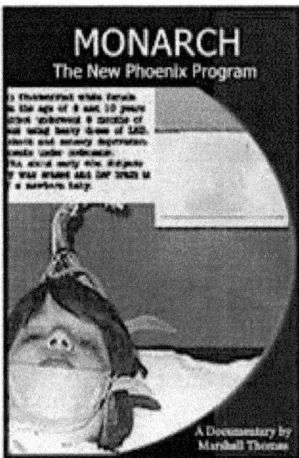

*The vast majority of Freemasons join and undergo rituals that seem to make no sense; it is only when one enters the highest levels, the circle within the circle if you like, that the secret knowledge of what this organisation and its rituals really are is revealed. This knowledge is communicated to a select few who reach 32° and beyond. What these rites and this organisation are has yet to be proven. **Freemasonry is one of the most important common threads linking victims of ritual abuse. These victims of ritual trauma often underwent MK-Ultra type experiments** [10] **in childhood. Thousands of people from different parts of the country, who have never been in contact with each other, all tell broadly the same story: that they were forced to take part in ritual abuse, including child rape and ritual sacrifice.** The consistency of these stories, the links between ritual abuse and MK-Ultra, seem at first to be fiction, but the victims' testimonies are very consistent and the involvement of high-degree Freemasons in these practices has been repeated many times. **Many of the personalities involved in the MK-Ultra***

---

[10] http://mk-polis2.eklablog.com/mk-ultra-p634125

*experiments were **High Freemasons**, such as **Dr Sidney Gottlieb**, **George Estabrooks**, **Ewen Cameron** and other members of the intelligence community. Freemasons have been accused of many things over the years, but it is likely that Freemasonry was infiltrated by members of the CIA, linked to MK-Ultra, in an effort to control this closed system and gain access to experimental subjects. The MK-Ultra programme was moved out of the laboratories into these closed systems of various types which could be manipulated and used to provide large numbers of children for mind control experiments and blackmail operations without directly involving the CIA."* (implied: Masonic networks would harbour children fractionated/dissociated by traumatic rituals)

The American survivor of the **MK-Ultra** programme, **Claudia Mullen**, who testified in 1995 before the Presidential Advisory Commission on Experiments Involving the Irradiation of Human Beings (as part of mental programming), **reported that she had attended parties in Masonic lodges when she was a child**. According to her, the *doctors* who worked on her as part of the MK-Ultra programme sent her to the Freemasons with the specific aim of **reinforcing her dissociative states** due to the extreme trauma they were subjecting her to.

She describes paedocriminal orgies within the Lodge itself:

*"They knew about my dissociative faculties from the start and they exploited it to the full. Because the more you split/dissociate, the easier it is for them to hide what they're doing. They created the traumatic circumstances necessary for dissociation, in particular by sending me to a Masonic lodge for a 'party'. They sent me there knowing that something horrible was going to happen to me... They knew then that I was going to split/dissociate... The first thing I remembered was incest, incestuous things at home... Then I gradually began to remember the rituals... I went to two Masonic 'parties' in a lodge. **These people go crazy at these parties, they get drunk... They make you spin... It's horrible what they do... They'd make you do sexual things, but they'd also make you watch other people doing it. Anything you can imagine, even with animals... and you had to watch it... It's as traumatic as going through it yourself. You're a child, and you have to stand there and watch a kid half your age being tortured or raped, etc....***

It's as traumatic as going through it yourself. Then they give you a choice: you can take their place... You have to decide whether it will be you or her... and if you decide not to, you have to live with the guilt that it happened to the other person because you decided it would. Either way, they've got you... You're generally screwed, there's no way out of this kind of situation". (Interview with Claudia Mullen, Wayne Morris, CKLN-FM - Mind Control Series Part 7)

 Australian **Kristin Constance** has publicly testified that she was a victim of ritual abuse and mind control. Her tormentors were none other than her own grandparents, founders of a women's Masonic lodge *of the Order of the Eastern Star.* Here is what she said at a conference organised by the S.M.A.R.T. group in 2011:

*"My grandfather was a 33rd degree Freemason and belonged to several lodges. He and my grandmother had founded a lodge of the Order of the Eastern Star in the suburbs of Sydney. I was in therapy for 20 years... The most difficult part of my recovery was to heal from a mental programming based on colours and on exploiting the left or right side of my body. This programming regularly caused me to dissociate (...) My first psychiatrist diagnosed me with borderline personality disorder. But she quickly corrected the diagnosis to Dissociative Identity Disorder (D.I.D.) when alter personalities began to emerge (...) My sister, who is 7 years older than me, also remembers suffering ritual abuse. One day, when I was 26, **she asked me if I remembered the underground chambers, and I told her I did... She then asked me if I remembered the screaming children, and I replied***

that I didn't, but that I knew they were there in other rooms (...) *17 years ago, when I confronted my mother and father about the ritual abuse, my mother told me that she wasn't involved in it, but she gave me the suitcase with all my grandfather's Masonic paraphernalia. She apologised for not being a good mother to me. I think that's the only answer I'll ever get from her about ritual abuse. That suitcase confirmed a lot of things for me. There were papers with passwords, hand signs and information about Masonic rituals. There were also the aprons, jewellery and medals that my grandfather and grandmother wore to meetings* (...)

I remember being put in cages, I remember electric shocks, scarifications, rapes, photos taken, drugs, hypnosis, food/light/oxygen/sleep deprivation. I was also locked in a coffin with spiders. I took part in rituals both indoors and out in nature. I was tied to altars. I took part in death and rebirth simulacra. I remember underground trap doors in the halls and being woken up countless times in the middle of the night to be taken to rituals. I was slashed, pierced and pricked so that my blood could be used in the rituals (...) *The colour programming I underwent took place in underground chambers. Each room had a different colour, corresponding to different programming. The colours seemed to correspond to those of the Eastern Star: blue, yellow, white, green, red and black for the centre. The red room had a red light, a stretcher, a table full of torture instruments and electro-shock equipment. In this room, the right side of my body was covered while the left side was subjected to electrical torture. Electrodes were placed on my joints, causing a paralysing pain that I still feel today. Things were whispered*

in my left ear and electric shocks were applied to my temples (...) In the blue room, there was a blue light, a stretcher, electro-shock equipment, buckets and a sink. The left side of my body was covered, and it was the right side that received electric shocks. Here the shocks were applied to my muscles (...) Red is about sexual slavery and blood rituals. I don't know whether everyone programmed by Freemasons receives this type of colour-based protocol. I suspect that depending on personality type, certain colours will be accentuated and worked on more than others. Perhaps birth dates influence the colours chosen. I don't understand what they're trying to do or create... I really wonder what the guideline is behind all this." (Kristin Constance - *Alleged Ritual Abuse by Freemasons and Order of the Eastern Star in Australia* - S.M.A.R.T. 2011)

Dissociative Identity Disorder (D.I.D.), or the splitting of the personality into multiple alterations, is deliberately provoked by traumatic rituals aimed at mental control. According to the *Diagnostic and Statistical Manual of Mental Disorders* (DSM), I.D.D. involves *"the presence of two or more distinct identities or 'personality states' that alternately take control of the subject's behaviour, accompanied by an inability to recall personal memories."* The cause is almost always a major childhood trauma. Patients typically present with dissociative amnesia, also known as **Traumatic Amnesia**. A closer look at I.D.D. shows that the natural dissociative and amnesic functions of the human mind can be exploited to manipulate and exploit the individual. **This is a veritable parallel psychiatric science, which in the wrong hands becomes a traumatic science and a weapon of undetectable mental control.** If this split personality disorder, with its amnesiac walls, is not taught - or only rarely - in medical faculties, and if it is systematically controversial and discredited by an elite of *experts*, it is for the simple reason that it is the main axis of the mind control practised by certain dominant occult organisations.

Michaela Huber
Psychologische Psychotherapeutin & Supervisorin

German psychotherapist **Michaela Huber** describes the mental programming methods used on children who have been dissociated by repeated extreme trauma: "*We found that many aggressors went so far as to torture children, using methods such as hunger, thirst, confinement, extreme pain with electric shocks and needles stuck everywhere. I don't want to go into detail here. A colleague once said that **these groups practise "unfettered physical terror", in other words, torture. The specific aim of this is to divide / split up children. The child then enters a dissociative state. You can see this very quickly when the child's eyes become glassy, shut or lost in a void... The pain disappears and the child freezes and relaxes. This is how these criminals create certain alter personalities (T.D.I.)**".* (*Wir sind die Nicki(s)* - ze.tt, 2020)

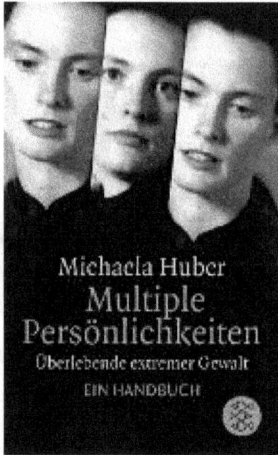

Michaela Huber
Multiple
Persönlichkeiten
Überlebende extremer Gewalt
EIN HANDBUCH

In one of her books, Michaela Huber defines trauma-based mind control as follows: *"Programming in the context of trauma is a process that can be described as learning under torture. The metaphor 'programming' is certainly of computer origin and in this context represents what psychologists call conditioning. This means that the person who has been "programmed" must react in a stereotyped way to certain stimuli. In this case, the person's reaction to a stimulus is automatic, so it is neither a natural reflex nor a conscious, voluntary reaction. To achieve his ends, the programmer, whom I'll call the torturer, used the fact that his victim was a young child, preferably already dissociated, with a split personality, to carry out the learning process by torturing him.* Torture can include physical, sexual and emotional abuse, and the victim is often threatened with death if they do not obey. Once a victim has been programmed, it is possible to control them using the stimuli that have been 'implanted' in them".* ("Multiple Persönlichkeit, Überlebende extremer Gewalt", Ein Handbuch - Fischer)

In 2009, **Dr Lowell Routley** described this type of mind control at a conference in Geneva at the annual international congress of the *ICSA* (*International Cultic Studies Association*). Here is an extract from the introduction: *"These survivors learned to dissociate themselves at a very young age through certain transgenerational practices transmitted within families. **The use of traumatic socialisation is designed to compartmentalise the child's mind, maintain secrecy and maintain the status quo.**"*

Asphyxiation, deprivation, isolation and pain are known to dissociate the child, ensure behavioural conformity, suppress autonomy and identity, create amnesia about abnormal activities and unquestioning loyalty (...) terror maintains and reinforces dissociative compartmentalisation. The degree of dissociation that results in the victim's mind is determined by the age at which this traumatic socialisation occurred, its frequency and intensity". (Restoring The Lost Self: Finding Answers to Healing from Traumatic Socialization and Mind Control in Twenty-first Century Neurocognitive Research)

Canadian **Lynn Moss-Sharman**, survivor and founder of the association and newspaper of the same name "*The Stone Angels*", spokesperson for ACHES-MC Canada (*Advocacy Committee for Human Experimentation Survivors & Mind-Control*), stated in an interview with Wayne Morris in 1998 that **Freemasonry is a common denominator in testimonies of ritual abuse and mind-control**: "*We realised that a large percentage of the victims had also been involved in Masonic ritual abuse. Their fathers or grandfathers were Freemasons or Shriners (Scottish Rite) in different parts of the country. We started to look at this much more closely because there seemed to be a common denominator. There had been hearings in Washington in 1995 and survivors of childhood mind control experiments had given*

evidence, so it became a public record. We were then able to publicly present information on the mind control practices that had been described by some of the survivors... The connection with the military began to be made, and once again **Freemasonry was a common denominator.** *Research by Dr Stephen Kent, a sociologist at the University of Alberta who studies occult practices and deviant religions, has shown that Freemasonry seems to be the secret society that comes up again and again when these occult activities* *are exposed in the testimonies of victims or investigators. We put forward this information about Freemasonry, and we paid for it in many ways (...) There were conversations about it that took place at meetings, the fear was about this Masonic connection. I put a few small ads in the 'Globe & Mail' about this as well as announcing forthcoming conferences. These few words about the Masonic connection generated phone calls and letters from victims all over Canada.* **People who described themselves as survivors of Masonic ritual abuse, still living in terror. They were always daughters of Scottish Rite Masons, daughters of Shriners. From the four corners of Canada, these people began to testify about memories of what could be described as experimentation on mind control.** *This began to manifest itself in November 1994. When the Thunder Bay conference attracted media attention - indeed there was a lot of media coverage for the event - Premier Bob Rae received faxes from Freemasons across the province complaining about what The Stone Angels were doing in Thunder Bay (...) there was a public outcry from the Freemasons because they were not allowed to attend our conferences...* (Interview with Lynn Moss Sharman, Wayne Morris, CKLN-FM - Mind Control Series Part 16)

The following information is taken from a summary of **Ann-Marie Germain**'s dissertation *"Ritual Abuse, Its Effects and the Process of Recovery Using Self Help Methods and Resources and Focusing on the Spiritual Aspect of Damage and Recovery"*, presented on March 30, 1993 at Southern Illinois University in Carbondale (USA): *"**My father was a 32nd degree Freemason and a Shriner.** Most of the conversations between him and me as adults took place between 1974 and 1977; here is an extract*:

Him (the father): *They do things in temples that can't be done in a lodge.*

Me (Ann-Marie): *What's wrong with that? What kind of things?*

Him: *I can't tell you... They do bad things and everything is kept secret.*

Me: *What's wrong, Dad?*

Him: *I'm sorry, Ann... I'm so sorry. I didn't know. I had no idea. I didn't know how bad it was.*

Me: *Sorry for what?*

Him: *You really don't remember? No ?*

Me: *Well, I don't know what to say, because I don't know what you're talking about...*

Later :

Him: *I need you to forgive me...*

Me: *Why?*

Him (with tears in his eyes): *I can't tell you...*

We may think that the father, sworn to Masonic secrecy, could not reveal these things to make amends, until his daughter herself had become aware of them by accessing her traumatic (amnesic) memories. Ann-Marie Germain recounted some of the traumatic memories that came back to her: "***Last year, during medium treatment for inflammation of my right eye, a memory came back in which my assailants were poking me in the eye and telling me that they had taken it out and would not put it back in until I pledged perpetual obedience to the 'Penis God'*** (phallic worship). ***I'd already seen eyeballs disappear and I knew they weren't joking... so I promised.***" Ann-Marie Germain also described a traumatic memory of being at the bottom of a grave as a child... or a ritual involving chanting, hooded robes, incense and torches.

Lynn Brunet's testimony is particularly interesting because it puts her finger on the question of the **dual personality of the abusers** who practise traumatic rituals and mind control on children. **Her father, himself a Freemason and Rosicrucian, abused her when she was very young**. Here are a few extracts from her testimony: *"As the years passed, I remembered my father's sexual abuse when I was a child (...) I also discovered that sexual abuse and incest were woven throughout the family history over at least three generations (...).(...) From the outside, my family seemed quite normal, but the accumulated weight of this family history, full of trauma and tension, was a heavy* *burden for each generation to bear (...) Over the last few years, as the riddles of my own experience were resolved, I tried to talk to them about what I remembered. Fortunately for me, my mother was able to remember the night my father raped me at the age of four and so validate her daughter's statements. However, the ritual abuse was beyond their comprehension, which is understandable in many ways. In mid-2004, my father began to develop Alzheimer's disease. During the initial period of the disorder, in an altered state of consciousness, he began to talk to me about the darker side of his Masonic involvement. He confessed to me that he was aware of the existence of certain groups who used Masonic rituals in violent contexts to initiate children. He told me: "There are a lot of these groups, a lot of people know about them, but they don't talk about it because it's embarrassing".*

His conversations with me alternated between coherent ones in which he told me about his involvement with other men in these groups. Sometimes in the evening, he would manage to get out of the retirement home and he would start climbing trees like a soldier on a mission to, he believed, observe the activities of the cult in order to "get the children out of the cult". This "strategic mission" lasted for a fortnight until he thought he had got all the children back. After that he seemed to be very satisfied with what he had achieved and all signs of his inner turmoil calmed down (...) The memories concerning the irregular Masonic activities were clearly to be attributed to a certain part of his psyche which is not normally accessible to consciousness and they had perhaps at that time become intertwined with his war experiences. It is possible that by raising this question I had

*plunged my father into an inner conflict, his memory loss having begun just after my confrontation with him. However, his brief period of honesty with me undoubtedly contributed to a mutual healing process. This confession, combined with the knowledge of the Masonic Order that I have been able to acquire, has refocused my attention away from anger at the man himself. **I am now led to understand the principles behind these age-old 'magical' practices, which divide the psyche of these men into two: on the one hand, dedicated citizens and men, and on the other, the most puerile, absurd and cruel of human creatures"**.* (Terror, Trauma And The Eye In The Triangle - Lynn Brunet, 2007) - **Dr. Jekyll & Mr Hyde** -

The psyche divided in two or the **Way of the Chameleon**, the animal that changes colour according to its environment. This is linked to **the phenomenon of multiple personality**, where the individual is able to adapt to different situations with different alter personalities. The public, benevolent facade is unaware (separated by amnesiac walls) of the occult activities of the alter personalities sitting in the depths of the internal system.

Survivors of mind control often report that their families (usually of high social standing) lead a perfectly normal and respectable public life, with the father of the family having a particularly adorable public persona, while at the same time slumbering within him a personality that could not be more sadistic or criminal...

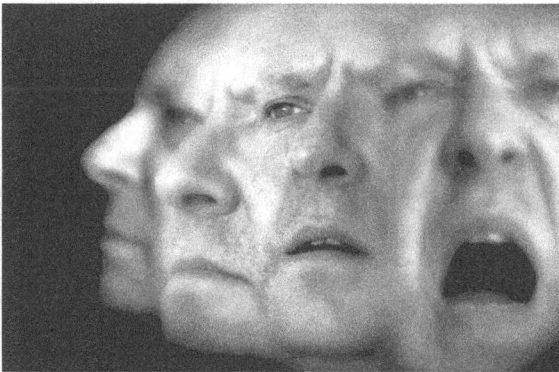

This is the case of **Cisco Wheeler**, a collaborator of Fritz Springmeier, whose father - a 33rd degree Freemason - had a resplendent external image, loving his family and doing a good job in the army. But in private, her father turned out to be a fearsome torturer who practised mental programming through trauma on his own offspring... According to her, he was himself *"multiple programmed"*, meaning that he had suffered extreme traumas as a child, deliberately provoked to split his personality: *"From my early childhood, I was trained to serve as a sex slave to the so-called 'elite' of political life (...) My father was a genius, but he was also a genius.... My father was a genius in every way, he had a kind side... He was a Satanist and a musician. He worked for the CIA and was a 33rd degree Freemason. By the way, there are still many degrees above that! He was a prisoner, as I was...*

Deep down, there was a moment in his life when he really knew what he was doing. On the outside, my father was very good.

He loved his family, he did a good job in the army, he loved people and people loved him. But I think there was a turning point in his life when he became aware of who he was and what he was really doing in secret. Certain internal barriers broke down, to the point where he finally realised... But I think he thought it was completely beyond him. It would have cost him his life to change direction. He had gone too far... " (Interview with Cisco Wheeler, Wayne Morris, CKLN-FM - Mind Control Series Part 22)

Kathleen Sullivan, a survivor of ritual abuse and mind control, describes in her autobiography the radical personality changes (dissociative states) her parents experienced when they mistreated their daughter: *"Every time, she used a white sheet to hang me from a beam.* **When she did that, her voice became that of a little girl.** *She seemed to be re-enacting what someone had done to her when she was a child.* **Then, strangely, her voice became that of an elderly person saying horrible things about me** *(...) On several occasions, she also locked me in a wooden box in the basement. Sometimes I would spend hours locked in pain inside this cramped box. When she came down to fetch me, she would "rescue me" from the box and ask me how I got there.* **She didn't seem to remember and I couldn't tell her that she was responsible** *(...) Dad, who was an electrical engineer, used some of his power tools to torture me in the basement. At times like that, his voice and facial expressions would change. He'd smile strangely and his voice would go up about half an octave. Even though he was hurting me badly, I felt protective of him, because he wasn't an adult any more. In each of these traumatic situations, **the telling factor was that my parents***

became like amnesiac strangers. They did things they didn't seem to remember afterwards. That's why I think both my parents had alter personalities committing acts they weren't fully aware of." (Unshackled: A Survivor's Story of Mind Control - Kathleen Sullivan, 2013)

In an interview with Jeff Wells published in 2005, Kathleen Sullivan, who was sexually exploited, said: "*I know several politicians who, in private,* **regressed into child alter personalities** *(...) At that point, their vocabulary became more simplistic and they used more concrete rather than abstract thinking.* **Their voices and faces also became younger. I didn't like it when they flipped like that, because these alter children were brutal and sadistic. They were more likely to lose control of themselves and do particularly horrible things to me. In those moments, they would forget who I was and treat me as if I were a woman from their past lives whom they hated."*

These statements corroborate the testimonies of certain luxury prostitutes reported in Sam Janus' book "*A sexual profile of men in power*". This study is based on more than seven hundred hours of interviews with luxury call-girls on the East Coast of the United States, **whose clients were prominent representatives from the worlds of politics, business, law and justice.** Most of them were adepts of *"highly perverse sexuality"* of the sadomasochistic and scatophilic type. **According to the prostitutes interviewed, many of these extremely influential and ambitious men literally regressed to an infantile stage following the sessions. For example, they wanted to be held, suckled and treated like babies...** (*"For a psychology of the future"* - Stanislav Grof, 2009)

Survivor **Bryce Taylor**, author of the book *"Thanks for the Memories"*, reports that her abuser of a father also had a completely unsuspected front personality. Outwardly, he behaved like a charming man, but no one would have suspected what he could do in private, the torture he inflicted on his children in order to split them up and programme them. **He himself suffered from severe dissociative disorders**: *"I think my father became a 'multiple programmer' as a result of the horrible satanic rituals he was subjected to. But I don't think he was aware of what he was doing when he programmed me, as not all the parts (alter) were aware of the totality of his*

*actions. I know he had a **multiple personality**... I've seen him switch between **child personalities** and all sorts of entities over the years.*" (Interview with Brice Taylor, Wayne Morris, CKLN-FM - Mind Control Series Part 23)

Clinical psychologist **Ellen Lacter**, based in San Diego, California, said in 2008: "*I've heard some incredible stories about Freemasonry, a lot of horrific abuse seems to happen in Masonic lodges. There are obviously many powerful individuals who are connected to Freemasonry and I believe that a lot of ritual abuse happens within the lodges themselves. Now I'm not saying that all Freemasons practice these horrors, I don't think so. In fact, I have no way of knowing whether the ritual abuses that occur in Masonic lodges are in some way part of the very structure of Freemasonry, or whether they are the result of individuals using this structure for their own purposes. **The fact remains that many victims, in my view very credible, claim that their attackers were prominent Freemasons**.*"

In August 2007, **Samantha Cooper** gave public testimony at the tenth annual meeting of the S.M.A.R.T. group. This survivor of domestic ritual abuse and mind control has been diagnosed with dissociative identity disorder. Here are a few extracts from her testimony:

"My paternal grandfather, my great-grandfather, my father and my uncle were high-grade Freemasons. My memories of sectarian experiences are centred on these people. My brother, sister and I were involved in cult rituals. There was incest with the parents, but close relatives were also aggressors, and there was also child pornography. My mother's behaviour was totally erratic, and it was extremely difficult to live with her because her psychology was so unstable and unpredictable. My father was away from home most of the time. When he was present, his

behaviour fluctuated from a very energetic and attentive attitude to one of withdrawal, distancing and silence, as if he was no longer aware of things around him (...) I think the mind control protocols began when I was about five years old. I think my parents were paid to put my sister and me, who were already dissociated, through these programmes (...)

*The feelings of fear and shame that are attached to the memories and threats inflicted on the child I was, are very dissuasive elements that made me bury these memories in myself even more. There were statements like "**No one will believe you**" or "**You'll look like a madwoman and they'll lock you up for ever**"; "**You know we control this place**", etc.* Another threat was that if I ever did anything again, I'd **be locked up.** *Another threat was that if I ever talked about it or remembered it, I would "shatter **into a million pieces and no one would ever be able to put me back together again**", a convincing argument for a child already internally polyfragmented by trauma (...) The fear was first instilled in me by my parents, then reinforced by my traumatic*

experiences in the sect, and finally refined and regulated by the programmers and their mind control. They take advantage of a child's lack of understanding and knowledge to manipulate and exploit them (...) **I simply had no feeling, or memory, of having been a child** *(...)* **The only way I know of to manage dissociation and heal from childhood trauma is to process traumatic memories so that they become normal memories with a rough chronology. I build bridges between my childhood past and my adult present** .

In England, we have **Aria**'s testimony about the involvement of members of the British police in organised child sex abuse. In London in the 1990s, **Aria recounts being forced by her father to take part in ceremonies at Masonic lodges, where she was ritually abused along with other children**. Aria speaks of several places where the abuse took place, including a shop in Brighton and a flat above *Russel & Bromley*'s shoe shop in Richmond, London. Her father and uncle, both Freemasons, actively participated in rituals specifically designed to traumatise / fragment the children and prevent them from speaking. Survivor Aria also talks in her testimony about the ritual killing of an animal and, according to her, a child. She describes some of the techniques used by these occult groups to traumatise and control their young victims:

"I remember a lot of strange abuse at these meetings, which were like parties for them.... This was before I was 12 (...) *Something else happened with this Masonic group, in another place where I remember being taken one evening with other children. There was a swimming pool there. There, I underwent a drowning exercise. They threw me into the pool, tied me up, and my father came to "save" me so that he could establish himself as a "trustworthy person" even though he was responsible for the abuse* (...) **I just remember sinking to the bottom of the water and entering a state of timelessness. I was there, it was like an eternity. The notion of time was distorted, I just remember that at one point... I had to choose between staying alive or dying. But it seemed very peaceful on the other side, everything seemed much more peaceful than existence on this earth** (...) *I also remember being taken by my father to be a prostitute. There were lots of naked little boys and girls. They put dog leads round their necks and took them to disgusting little rooms where people - sick people - would come and pay... This was above the Russell & Bromley shoe shop in Richmond. I had the impression that my father was using me to earn money, and there were other parents who took their children there for the same reasons. I think they're sick and have no empathy. They're focused on money and power.* **The deeper reason is that they probably went through the same conditioning as children, they**

were abused so much that they don't remember those awful sensations. So they're just repeating the abuse to the next generation. I think they have completely detached themselves from the feeling of being a little child. They have totally identified themselves as abusers (...) I was also abused at the Brighton Masonic Lodge (...) There was one in Surbiton, one in Brighton and the big lodge in central London, where I have another extreme memory. It's right in the centre of town, I think it's the main lodge in London. There was a ceremony going on, mostly little boys and me. They were all wearing their stupid Masonic costumes. **During this ceremony with the consumption of blood, an animal was sacrificed on an altar. The worst thing about this ritual was the way the sacrifice was carried out. They wanted all the children to come together to stab the poor little boy in the heart and kill him... So they want to make you feel guilty. They want the child to think he's an executioner himself. They want to burden you with guilt so that you are afraid to speak out. You are suddenly made to take part in something that you would absolutely never want to do. This creates a lot of doubts and prevents you from speaking out... You feel as if you've become an abuser yourself. On the same day, during this ceremony, the Freemasons got together with the little boys and with me. They went to different rooms behind the altar, at the back of the building, to assault and rape. My uncle was also there, and it was he who took me to a room to rape me. It was normal for** them...". (*Aria speaks out about ritual abuse* - karmapolice.earth, 2019)

The American activist and survivor of ritual abuse and mind control, **Jeanette Westbrook,** has publicly reported the ritual abuse to which she is alleged to have been subjected by her father. Her father was a senior civil servant and director of the US National Board of Boiler and Pressure Vessel Inspectors. In this position, he supervised inspections of all the nuclear power plants in the United States. **He was a Freemason initiated** into *the Jeffersontown* **Masonic Lodge #774 in Kentucky**. Here's what Westbrook said publicly about his father:

"In the case of this particular lodge, I believe there is some evidence because two other cases have been tried and there have been convictions. Two assailants were linked to the same Masonic Lodge, of which my assailant father had also been a member for over 30 years... Is there a correlation here? Yes, because like attracts like (...) My father's last attack took place at the age of 24. This happened from early childhood until the age of 24. The memory recovery process was very slow. You only remember certain incidents, or you only have flashes like a film viewed from a distance, sometimes with very clear images, sometimes blurred... I really started to have a lot of memories and flashes from the age of 28 when I met and married my husband (...) There were different types of abuse... Here's a very

vivid and clear memory, which I drew, but which I also told the police inspector when I lodged a complaint against my father: **I was hung upside down with ropes, in a garage near our house. I still have scars on my ankles...** *I was also threatened with a soldering iron, or hung upside down and penetrated with an object...* **Other times I was woken up in the middle of the night to be taken who knows where and raped...** *It could be at any time of night, with people I knew or didn't know (...)*

When I spoke to someone in my father's family about this, she told me that she had been raped by two members of that family, who had also raped me when I was a child! **I was able to go back at least three generations... The police also had photographs and access to the site where I was taken as a child to be ritually abused. The evidence is there...** *Not only did my private detective investigate, but other police officers supported me and accompanied me to go before the prosecutor (...)* **I think that he and his brothers tried not only to pervert me, but also to break my spirit... to split my spirit into pieces, to divide my personality... My sister remembers my father calling me by different names, and she wondered why... He was clearly aware of my different alter personalities** *(...)* **I believe, and I'm even sure, that the organisations that we call Satanists, paedophile clubs, programmers, are very well informed about the defence**

system that is Dissociative Identity Disorder. They know it very well and they deliberately create it in order to conceal their perversions. They use it to protect their identity. So that I and all my alter personalities suffering horrific and sadistic abuse can get up in the morning to function normally, go to school and then come home to live with the abusers. The players behind the scenes - the District Attorney, the police officers handling my case, my lawyer and others in the Kentucky District Attorney's office - all knew that this was a case of ritual abuse... All these people were convinced because of the extensive evidence I had in my possession, but also with the support of the testimonies of the other victims..."

What Jeanette Westbrook describes here, when she states that her father called her by different names, corresponds to an individual - an initiate - who cultivates the dissociative states of his victim in a process of mental control. He thus reinforces the splitting of the personality (T.D.I.) created by the extreme traumas aimed at exploiting the different alter personalities.

We find this same protocol in Belgium in the testimony of Régina Louf, Witness X1 in the Dutroux **affair,** who was examined by a panel of five experts led by psychiatrist Paul Igodt, who concluded that Régina Louf did indeed suffer from a dissociative identity disorder as a result of massive sexual abuse.

In her autobiography *Silence on tue des enfants*, Louf describes how a certain Tony (Antoine Vanden Bogaert) had literally had his hands on her since early childhood, and how he set about exploiting her as a sex slave in an elitist paedophile ring. **Tony was obviously well aware of dissociative processes and even seemed to cultivate them in his slave:**

"In Knokke, at my grandmother's house, the adults noticed that I spoke with the voices in my head, that I quickly changed moods, or even that I sometimes spoke with a different voice or accent. Although I was only 5 or 6 years old, I realised that these things were strange and not allowed. So I learned to hide my inner voices, my other selves (...) **Tony was the only adult who understood that something was wrong in my head. It didn't bother him at all; on the contrary, he cultivated it. He gave me different names:** *Pietemuis, Meisje, Hoer, Bo.* **The names slowly became a part of me. The strange thing was that if he mentioned a name, the personality that matched the name was immediately called.** *"Pietemuis" (little mouse) became the name of the little girl he brought home after abuse - a frightened, nervous little girl he could comfort by talking to her in a caring, fatherly way. "Meisje' (girl) was the name of the part of me that belonged exclusively to him. If he abused me in bed early in the morning, for example, or if there was no one around. "Hoer" (whore) was the name of the part of me that worked for him. "Bo" was the young woman who looked after him if he got drunk and needed looking after.* **"Now you leave that to me,"** *he'd say when I asked him curiously why he gave me so many names, and he'd add:* **"Daddy Tony knows you better than you know yourself"**... *And it was sadly true.* **And it was sadly true.**

Who initiated this Tony on how to cultivate and exploit Regina Louf's I.D.T.? Where did he learn about these mind-control techniques? Is he himself a member of a secret society? Is he himself a victim with a split personality?

Passing through the mirror= dissociation

Extreme traumatic rituals are used to bring about this "*illumination*": the transcendence of the physical body through the dissociative phenomenon. The heart of Satanic perversion lies in "*tearing out the soul*" of the victim in order to vampirize his energy and control his mind. It's not the rituals themselves that really count, but rather their effects at levels beyond the material world...

In the document containing the hearings and minutes of the Dutroux case, already cited, we can read on page 261 the reproduction of a letter dated 1996 describing the paedocriminal sectarian practices of a group of notables:

Sects - Orgies - Pink ballets in Holland. Letter to the Dutch Justice Department about sects in Holland. There is a group of 300 people in Holland who form a sect. They organise orgies with minors (aged 3 and over).

Members = lawyers - jurists - judges - policemen... Meetings in country estates, hotels or at one of the members' homes (...) Meeting on the first Saturday after the full moon and on Christian feast days and birthdays. Groups of 12 people with *children. **Rape and torture of children. Large assemblies = 50 adults and 50 children - drugs, drinks, orgies, rape, video recording of child abuse. Children of group members take part in parties. This creates multiple personalities in the children.***

At Christmas, the sacrifice of a 1-year-old child is simulated. The child is abused but replaced by a doll when the real torture takes place. Simulated burial of a 15-year-old child as a punishment. **Multiple personalities are induced, for example, by making small children believe that a cat has been introduced into them, which grows into a panther that will watch them** *if they want to talk or leave the clan. These multiple personalities are maintained by clan psychotherapists. Induced multiple personalities allow continuous control, even of adults, by creating a certain balance. This turns all the perpetrators into victims...*

This brings us back to the notion of the splitting up of the personalities of the individuals involved in these elitist networks, who initiate their own descendants during traumatic rituals...

Robert Oxnam spent more than a decade at the head of the prestigious American cultural institution, the *Asia Society*. He is a member of *the* so-called '*elite*', rubbing shoulders with the likes of Bill Gates, Warren Buffet, George Bush, etc., **but he is also multiple...** in other words, his personality is split. He **has been diagnosed with dissociative identity disorder** and has written an autobiography entitled '*A Fractured Mind*'. In 2005, the *CBS News* programme *60 Minutes* did a feature on him to explain this particular mental disorder. Robert Oxnam had a very rigid upbringing and was under a lot of pressure to succeed socially and professionally. His father was a university president and his grandfather was a bishop and president of the World Council of Churches (WCC)... His grandfather was none other than **Garfield Bromley Oxnam**, an important representative of the American Protestant community, leader of the *American Methodist Church* and friend of evangelist Billy Graham, both of whom campaigned for a Christian liberalism aimed at establishing a *"One Church for One* World" world religion. **According to Fritz Springmeier, G. Bromley Oxnam and Billy Graham were 33rd degree Freemasons involved in Satanic ritual abuse and mind control...** John Daniel, in his book *"Two Faces of Freemasonry"*, states that grandfather Oxnam attained the 3rd degree at *Temple Lodge 47* in Greencastle on 22 November 1929 and received the 33rd honorary degree on 28 September 1949.

So we have Springmeier claiming in the 90s, according to his sources, that grandfather Oxnam was a high Masonic initiate involved in traumatic rituals... allegations never proven... **then, a decade later** (in 2006), **we have his grandson, Robert Oxnam, publicly revealing that he suffers from severe split personality... which is the typical symptom of the consequences of traumatic ritual abuse aimed at mind control.** Isn't this a strong indication that Springmeier's sources are reliable and that the Oxnam family would practise these horrors on their descendants? Robert Oxnam may well have undergone trauma-based programming. Following his brilliant studies, he was very quickly promoted in the major media and 'propelled' to a prestigious and elitist position...

Robert Oxnam was on the *top of the world*, but inside him there was a mixture of depression, anger and rage. **On the one hand, there was this glittering social and professional success, and on the other a permanent malaise and depression that was getting worse.** In the 1980s, Oxnam was treated for alcoholism and bulimia. Consultations with a psychiatrist for his addiction problems and **recurring memory lapses** did nothing to improve anything. He sometimes woke up with bruises and wounds all over his body, without any idea of what might have caused them, or even the context in which they might have happened. **He apparently had another life in parallel**... One day, he found himself lost in the crowd at Central Station in New York, in a trance-like state, and **he heard voices** harassing him, telling him that he was bad, that he was the worst person who had ever lived. In 1990, during a therapy session with Dr Jeffrey Smith, **Robert Oxnam suddenly became someone else... His psychiatrist reported a complete change in his voice, attitude and movements.** During one session, Dr. Smith reported that Oxnam's hands *were like claws*, he was in a terrible rage. This anger came from a little boy called '*Tommy*'. When Smith told Oxnam what had happened during the session, Oxnam said that he didn't know *Tommy* at all and had no recollection of what had happened in the therapist's office. It was then that Dr Smith realised that he might be dealing with a case of multiple personality.

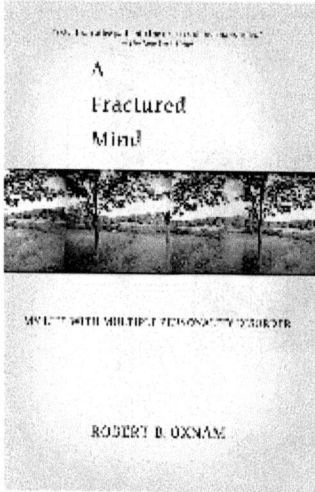

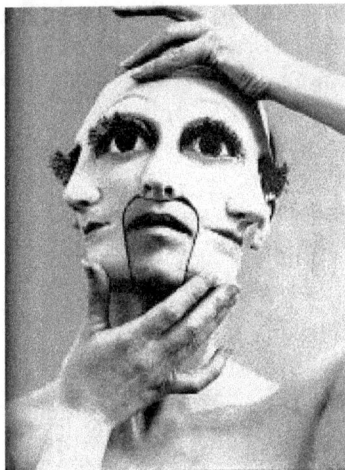

In the course of the therapy, **eleven very distinct alter personalities emerged independently of each other.** They included *Tommy*, an angry young boy, the *Witch*, a terrifying alter, and *Bobby and Robby*. *Bob* was the dominant personality, in other words the host personality: the public face, in this case an intellectual working at the *Asia Society*. In his public life, Robert Oxnam went about his business, meeting with dignitaries such as the Dalai Lama. **But this public life gave no hint of his profound personality disorders...** During his therapy, an alter named *Baby* brought back **memories of childhood abuse. These involved severe sexual and physical abuse,** always accompanied by the words: "*You're bad, this is punishment*".

Did Robert Oxnam experience Masonic ritual abuse? Did he undergo intentional personality splitting as a child? Did he belong to one of those elitist families who practise systematic mental control over their offspring? Where did the terrifying '*Witch*' alter come from? In any case, his case clearly demonstrates how **an individual can have a dissociative**

identity disorder while conducting business at a high level and maintaining a perfectly normal public façade. Is this what Fritz Springmeier is referring to when he speaks of *slaves under totally undetectable mental control*, to describe these **voluntarily split and programmed** individuals? ("*A Fractured Mind: My Life with Multiple Personality Disorder*" - Robert B. Oxnam, 2006)

It would appear that the traumatic initiation of children into certain lodges is intended to create a pool of individuals who are more or less mentally programmed and therefore able to serve Masonic projects in the near future. In adolescence and adulthood, the child who has undergone ritual abuse - and the mental control that goes with it - will receive all the support and money needed from the network to be strategically injected into society, where he or she will appear with a front personality (*Dr Jekyll*). The aim is to place 'safe' individuals in key positions, as 'weak links' are out of the question in such a system of global control.

On the subject of the *"Masonic-Schizo"* double life, the case of a prominent person with a suspected split personality was reported by Dr. Richard Kluft in his book *Childhood Antecedents of Multiple Personality*. Dr. Kluft describes the story of a 22-year-old man who was subjected to a psychiatric examination by a judge, at which time the possibility that he was suffering from dissociative identity disorder was considered. The man was on trial for the murder of his father . He told police that his father

CBS News
Dr. Richard Kluft

was a well-known pharmacist and a 'pillar' of the local community, but that he was involved in drug dealing and had connections with organised crime. Based on statements from the defendant, his family and his wife, it was found that the father was also very likely to have a dissociative identity disorder. He was described as an unpredictable man who went into inappropriate rages with voice changes and unusual behaviour. Both the defendant and some of his family members reported that the father acted as *if he* were *"two different people"*, claiming that he was both a *"drug dealer"* and a *"pillar of the community"* - that is to say, he had an occult criminal activity on the one hand and a very respectable public front on the other - Dr Jekyll & Mr Hyde. Mr Hyde - History does not tell us whether he was a Freemason, but his status as a notable pharmacist and "pillar of his community" suggests that he belonged to a lodge of some kind.

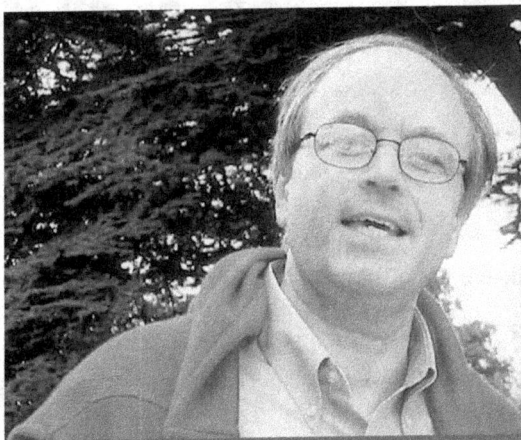

We can also mention **Jacques Heusèle**, another case of a notable who led an extremely compartmentalised double life. A **Freemason** and a devoted member of the **Rotary Club**, Heusèle was a prosperous insurance agent in Arras who led a double life that was completely unknown to those close to him. A parallel existence linked to a prostitution ring, and probably to the organisation of pink ballets (paedocriminality)... **It was only**

after his death (murder) **that his family discovered and understood who he really was** - Dr Jekyll & Mr Hyde -...

However, history does not tell us whether Heusèle suffered from a split personality or dissociative identity disorder. It should be remembered that it was in this case that the lawyer Bernard Méry heard a judge retort to him: "*Maître, there is nothing we can do in this case, you have Freemasonry... What do you want to do about Freemasonry?*

In England, we have the *Waterhouse* affair (also known as the *Lost in Care* or *North Wales child abuse scandal*). This is one of the UK's biggest child abuse scandals. Dozens of former residents of children's homes in Wales told investigators about appalling abuse: "*serious and systematic abuse*", according to the police.

One of the many victims, **Keith Gregory**, suffered two years of psychological, physical and sexual abuse as a child at *Bryn Estyn*'s home. Keith Gregory, now a Wrexham councillor, **said he was regularly taken from the home by staff to a hotel where he was sexually abused by groups of men and that this was an elitist paedophile ring.** Lonely children from care homes have always been targets for these horror networks... (see the similar case of the Jersey orphanage "*Haut de la Garenne*")

Keith Gregory

Keith Gregory told *BBC5* Radio that he was convinced the abusers escaped justice **because of their "*Masonic connections*".** He claims that politicians, judges and police chiefs accused of raping children in these orphanages in Wales escaped justice because most of them were Freemasons...

Bill Brereton, then Deputy Chief Constable of North Wales Police, strongly recommended that an **external and independent investigative body** should **be able to determine whether a Masonic Network could have protected the Freemason paedophiles involved in this case**... a request which was quickly rejected by his superiors. Furthermore, when the victims' lawyer, Nick Booth, tried to put forward the "*Masonic Factor*", he was quickly reprimanded for questioning the integrity of Sir Ronald Waterhouse's court... himself a Freemason. When Nick Booth simply asked Judge Waterhouse to determine whether any of the investigators, lawyers or witnesses connected with the case were Freemasons, this transparency was rejected without any justification... Booth then explained that "**a *Brother Mason*'s duty of loyalty and his duty of impartiality if he is involved in the administration of justice, must be put on public record.**"

Sir Ronald Waterhouse

Published in 2000, the Waterhouse Commission's investigation, which focused on the abuse that took place within the homes themselves, concluded that there was no evidence to support any large-scale protection or paedophile criminal network. For Waterhouse, all these rapes of minors were isolated cases, and of course no public figures were involved... While the Commission was asked to determine the nature of the "*dysfunctions*" in certain orphanages in Wales, it set out to systematically dismantle the accusations of the victims, **who denounced an organised system that went beyond the framework of the homes.**

Did the Waterhouse Commission suppress essential evidence to cover up a network?

When you consider that Freemasons swear an oath to protect their *Brethren* whatever happens, the integrity of the courts is greatly called into question, i.e. the judiciary and the upper hierarchy of the forces of law and order are largely, if not totally, subject to the Lodge (under Masonic oath)...

The institutional sphere capable of applying real Justice: judges, lawyers, senior police or gendarmerie officers are for the most part currently connected or directly initiated into this network of Masonic secret societies. This is one of the reasons why it is so difficult today to obtain prosecutions in this type of case. **The institutions of 'justice' with which you hope to protect children... in reality seem to be working against the interests of children, as numerous cases have shown...**

In 1990, in Evansville, Indiana (Vanderburg County, USA), a sordid case of paedophile rituals was hushed up, as usual. At the time, the so-called **"Satanic Blue House"** affair received national attention, notably with the television programme *A Current Affair*, which described Evansville as a "*Devil's Playground*".

In 2017, **Jon Pounders** of *NYSTV*, in collaboration with **David Carrico** (author of *The Egyptian Masonic Satanic Connection*), produced a documentary (*Dark Covenant - Secret of Secrets*) detailing the *Blue House* affair, which has received little or no reference in the French-speaking world. For legal reasons, the documentary does not mention the Masonic connection of this case, but the producers state off the record that the accused are all linked to Freemasonry.

Jon Pounders claims that *the people involved in this Blue House, in particular the school principal, whose name is most mentioned, but also civil servants, all these people involved in the abuse and the cover-up of the affair were Freemasons, without exception. They were all Freemasons, and the file is public.*

One of the victims testifies:

"When I was 8, they used to take me out of school... the headmaster would come into the classroom and tell the teacher that he was taking us to a special course to 'learn'. They would take us to this Blue House. We never got justice... The public prosecutor never launched an investigation despite all the overlapping testimonies. We didn't tell anyone about it because we were threatened with trouble too, because of everything we'd done... But we were just kids."

The Evansville children said they had been taken out of school to be subjected to **ritualised paedo-satanic violence** in what they called a Blue House. According to the victims, **these rituals involved sexual abuse as well as blood sacrifices**.

Lead children's advocate Rick Doninger said:

"All the children in the Blue House claimed to have been mistreated by Freemasons. The public prosecutor refused to open an investigation. Why did he do this? It's a mystery!

Rick Doninger - Child Advocate

Stan Levco
PROSECUTOR

Doninger also stated that the investigation had been entrusted to police officers who were also Freemasons...

The many overlapping testimonies, as well as **the medical and psychological examinations confirming the veracity of the abuse and trauma**, did not prevent prosecutor Stanley Levco from declaring to the "*Current Affair*" journalist that he did **not believe** the children's word and would therefore not open any investigation...

Despite extensive testimony and evidence, the case was never brought before a court and no arrests were made, leaving the little victims once again in the loneliness of injustice.

David Carrico- Author/ Researcher

David Carrico states that "*the most frustrating thing about this is that there were twelve children who were interviewed by **Bill Welborn** (former prosecutor) and by **Sue Donaldson** (head of the psychology department at the University of Evansville) who interviewed six of them: **these children all said the same thing,*** *without knowing each other, they all gave the same testimony. In particular, they mentioned two Freemasons who took them to this house for rituals... This was confirmed medically at the hospital, and the abuse was recognised. There's this child who claims that the principal raped her in his office with an object... This child was examined in hospital and the rape was medically confirmed! There are physical marks, there are multiple testimonies, but there is no prosecution!"*

Lawyer Bill Welborn reported in *Current Affair*: *"First of all, there were many children who reported very similar practices. The second thing is the similarity of the physical marks of abuse. Many of them were assaulted and injured in identical ways.*

The children reported being subjected to **electric shock sessions while viewing photos, with the aim of inverting good and evil by renaming the photo its exact opposite; just like putting their hand under hot water and telling them it was something cold for them.** *"We no longer knew right from wrong"*, some said. They said they were forced to look at dead, butchered animals in chests, forced to swallow their own vomit if they fell ill from eating the sacrificed animals. **Here we find occult rituals aimed at eliminating any notion of good and evil, confirming that these were practices inspired by a certain Gnosis specific to secret societies.**

Sue Donaldson, at the time a professor of psychology at the University of *Southern Indiana*, made public statements on the television programme *Current Affair*. She examined six of these children, and they all had similar scars: "*When I saw the first child, I wondered if he hadn't done it to himself. Once I saw the second, then the third, the fourth, etc, right up to the sixth, they all had these scars in the same place. They said they'd been cut in the Blue House by the teachers who'd taken them out of school.*"

After the psychological interviews and physical examinations, Sue Donaldson could no longer reject their words: "*Something has happened to these children*", she said. **It was obvious to her that these children had experienced trauma, but she didn't know exactly what it was. She confirmed that the children were severely traumatised...**

A member of the "*Children of the Underground*" child protection association helped one of these children (Sarah Jane Wannamaker) and her mother to flee to Altanta in order to escape

the custody of the allegedly abusive father . Sarah had made precise and detailed statements about satanic ritual abuse: murder, cannibalism, prayers to demons, threats to *cut her in half*, etc. At the time, this association member declared that Evansville would be a nest for transgenerational Satanists. The area is also known as a Masonic stronghold...

Sarah said that **the executioners filmed all their rituals, threatening the children with photos if they spoke out.** She mentioned an alleged child sacrificial murder perpetrated by the principal of the school (Shriners), who allegedly cut off the victim's legs. It was reported that little Sarah was possibly developing **dissociative identity disorder**, as she switched from one character to another while giving evidence. She described around twenty adults wearing blue or black hooded togas. She drew Egyptian symbols, similar to certain Masonic ornaments on large buildings in downtown Evansville. The girl claimed that they kept babies in jars and that **every act they performed on a child was recorded on a scroll.**

Almost every time a case of *"Satanic/Masonic ritual abuse"* is brought before the *courts*, the case is immediately dismissed as unfounded... This judicial lock-up could validate the existence of a power structure that goes beyond the official legal system. Is this the notion of *a state within a state* (or *deep state*) that Sophie Coignard denounced in her investigation into Freemasonry? Jon Pounders says on the subject: *"The problem is that when you have this kind of case where a Freemason protects a Freemason, where a judge is himself a Freemason, and so on, it's very difficult for a prosecutor or investigator to get to the bottom of it. Even a prosecutor or investigator who wants to move things forward sometimes can't. It's scary because a lot of these people - Freemasons - are police officers... In Evansville, Indiana, more than half of the police force is initiated into Freemasonry, so their Masonic oath trumps their oath to serve and protect the people. It's a big problem in politics too..."*

When confronted with the notions of Satanism/Luciferism, magic/sorcery, blood sacrifice, demonology, sexual magic, secret societies, etc., the atheist is faced with an ideological wall; he will then describe these supernatural questions as irrational, superstitious or archaic. They are intellectually/spiritually powerless to begin to understand paedocriminal ritual practices of the darkest occultism. It's a step that needs to be taken before we can begin to grasp this harsh reality...

Dr Stephen Kent said: *"I am most concerned about certain deviant groups within Freemasonry. To me, it's quite plausible to imagine deviant Freemasons drawing on some of Aleister Crowley's extremist writings or interpreting some of his statements about children and sex, or some of his claims about child or adult sacrifice, literally and incorporating them into their rituals."*

In his book *Do What You Will: A History of Anti-Morality*, Geoffrey Ashe writes that Aleister Crowley was *"like three or four different men"*.

Crowley himself described his altered states of consciousness in which he confronted other imaginary, dissociative or spiritual entities. Did Crowley himself have a multiple personality, a personality split by childhood trauma? Did he

have a dissociative identity disorder? In his book *Magick in Theory and Practice*, Crowley advocates self-punishment by scarification with a razor blade. Therapists who work with ritual abuse survivors report that self-harm by scarification is the most common feature of patients with severe dissociative disorders. The pain and endorphin release provided by scarification is a means - usually unconscious - of dissociating and relieving inner unhappiness.

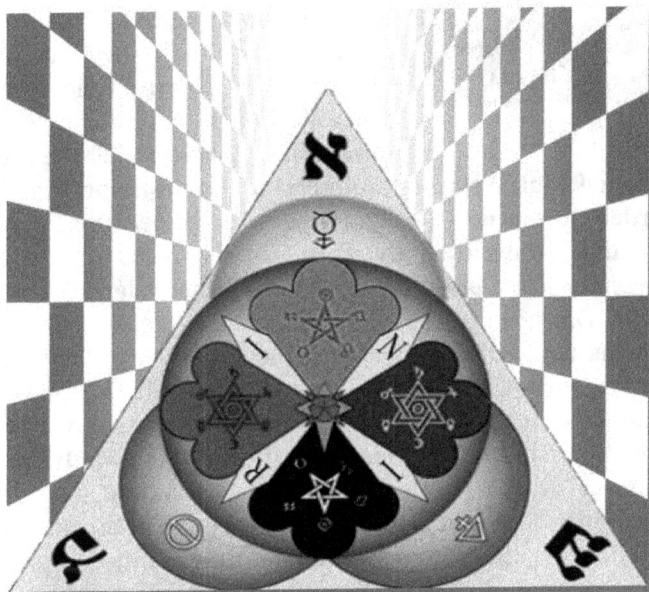

Aleister Crowley joined the *Hermetic Order of the* **Golden Dawn** in 1898, only to be expelled from the secret society in 1900. In 1901, a scandal hit the Golden Dawn when Theo Horos (Frank Jackson) and his wife were accused of raping a sixteen-year-old girl. At the time, **the judge concluded that the couple had used Golden Dawn rituals to sexually exploit minors**. According to Richard Kaczynski, author of *"Of Heresy And Secrecy: Evidence of Golden Dawn Teachings On Mystic Sexuality"*, **practices of sexual magic were commonplace within this secret society. Sexual magic is a common teaching in all these different Luciferian lodges.**

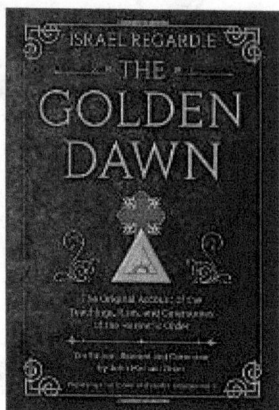

The Golden Dawn was created following the discovery of mysterious Germanic documents. These were coded manuscripts that were deciphered and transcribed by one of the founding members of the Order, Dr. William Wyn Westcott, a Freemason. The documents were subsequently suspected of being falsified, and in order to clarify the matter, the author of "*The Magicians of the Golden Dawn*", Ellic Howe, sent Westcott's translations to an expert in graphology. **The expert concluded that Westcott probably had multiple personality disorder (dissociative identity disorder) because of his distinctive handwriting styles.** In his book '*What You Should Know About The Golden Dawn*', Gerald Suster, a lawyer for the Golden Dawn, disputed the multiple personality disorder argument, noting that another prominent member of the Order, Israel Regardie, also had a writing style that could vary and that he had never been diagnosed with multiple personality or any psychiatric disorder... **One interpretation of these handwriting variations is that both men have dissociative disorders caused by traumatic ritual experiences. Therapists who specialise in dissociative disorders describe well how a change in writing style in the same person is a marker that can indicate shifts from one personality to another.** ("Cult & Ritual Abuse" - James Randal Noblitt & Pamela Perskin Noblitt, 2014, p.141)

- Dr Jekyll & Mr Hyde -

We have already mentioned the **Ordo Templi Orientis** (O.T.O.) and its occult practices of sexual magic. This secret society (a sub-structure of the Golden Dawn), which can be described as Masonic because it was founded by two Freemasons and is based on the same Gnostic schema and soil, has on several occasions been denounced **as a veritable paedocriminal network.**

Australian psychologist **Reina Michaelson,** who received an award in 1996 for her work on the prevention of sexual abuse of minors, **claims that in certain O.T.O. rituals, children are literally massacred.** The O.T.O. took Michaelson to court over these accusations and won the case.

Dr Reina Michaelson

The psychologist had stated, according to her sources, that this secret society was a *paedophile network,* some of whose members practise ritual abuse involving sexual magic, trauma-based mind control and the production of paedo-pornography. She also stated that *this satanic cult had a great deal of power because it was run by very powerful and influential families, and* implied that senior politicians and other television personalities were part of a high-level paedophile network covered up by the authorities.

In 1995, the O.T.O. was listed as a Luciferian sect in a parliamentary report by the commission investigating sects in France.

Grottaferrata e Frascati. Trovati i resti di decine di riti

one messe nere"

otessa di Satana riesce a fuggire

In his book *L'Enfant sacrifié à Satan (The Child Sacrificed to Satan)*, journalist **Bruno Fouchereau** writes: "*In Rome, Italy, the existence of an O.T.O. group practising child rape as part of its rituals was revealed, causing a scandal because the city's gilded youth took part, as well as* well-known *lawyers...*".

Bruno Fouchereau's investigation reports the testimony of **Samir Aouchiche**, a victim of a para-Masonic sect called "**Alliance Kripten**". Here is an excerpt from the book, which describes a Golden Dawn ceremony **involving children** and in which Aouchiche took part: "Finally, they arrived in the room. Once again, the decor has changed. The walls are now draped in black fabric, the neon lights are switched off and halogen lights illuminate the room indirectly. **A huge mauve triangle is drawn on the floor, and a sort of chequerboard has been placed in its centre. On either side of the triangle, two kinds of columns about two metres high stand like obelisks. One is black and**

Samir Aonchiche

L'Enfant sacrifié à Satan

white, the other red and green. At the back of the room, facing the entrance, on a sort of platform framed by four candelabras, are two large red and gold armchairs (...) **Five or six children are there**, some visibly accompanied by their fathers or close friends. A little boy of about six, who refused to let go of his father's hand, received a monumental slap that sent him rolling to the floor to the laughter of the adults, who were clearly delighted by the sight of this half-stunned boy (...) Samir couldn't believe his eyes! The adults are dressed very differently.

Most wear **big white sarees, some are green and red**. Others are **dressed all in leather** (...) Others are bare-chested **but**

wearing masks. There are about twenty of them in all, wearing a variety of outfits. All are huddled together near the small room adjoining the auditorium. In this case, it seems to serve as a cloakroom, as the men and women all come out wearing more or less bizarre outfits, even though they had entered in street clothes. Ajouilark is there too, **draped in a red saie. On his chest is a huge purple triangle edged in black and topped with a white cross. His face is masked**, but Samir knows his eyes too well not to recognise him (...) Mass music plays and the 'Emperor', followed by the Commander, makes her way to the dais. In the meantime, Steerlarow is busily preparing on silver platters large quantities of what Samir later learns is cocaine.

Samir Aouchiche

Ondathom grabs Samir's arm to guide him, the winning girls and the other children to the front of the stage, where everyone lines up. The adults spread out, with a sort of saucy good humour, on the sides of the triangle, facing the columns and the platform (...) **As the trays pass through the audience, Ondathom and the Chinese man ruthlessly undress the children. Some sobbed, others shielded their faces as if expecting to be hit at any moment** (...) Conversations were going well: a man wearing a red mask declares himself sensitive to Samir's buttocks, a woman dressed in a white saie has nothing but praise for Steerlarow's prizewinners (...) During the Emperor's speech, Ondathom, with a copper ciborium in his hand, **gave the children a sip of a bitter red liquid. They all quickly felt the same. Their heads were spinning. They don't lapse into unconsciousness, but they are suddenly caught up in a kind of fog. The adults can see the effects of the drug as the children slump on top of each other**. The Emperor continues: *"Commander, carry the banner to the east!"* Ajouilark takes the banner in question and places it on the east wall of the room. **It depicts a golden cross with a white T on its axis, which is also the centre of a six-pointed star made up of two triangles, one**

red, the other blue. *"Commander, carry the banner west!* The western flag is a gold triangle on a blue background with a red cross in the centre. Samir can see these banners as if through a fog at , but the symbols inscribed on them will mark his mind forever. The Emperor raises his arms to the sky and closes his eyes to concentrate (...) *"Infuse these young beings (the Emperor seems to bless the children) with vigour and purity, you who are the masters of the elemental powers you control, and may these young beings remain a true symbol of the inner and spiritual strength of our order."* **This ritual is one of those of the Golden Dawn and seems to be the one Samir has been subjected to most often.** Samir can hardly hear the Emperor's words any more; he feels like he's falling, like he's caught in a whirlpool. Everything is spinning, faces are blending together, and he can barely hear the Commander declaim: *"The bodies of these children are the bread we share. They conceal our bonds and, through our sexuality finally liberated from the yoke of Judeo-Christian oppressors, we purify ourselves, reintegrating the sacred plane of the celestial knights of the Order of the Kripten Alliance. Sex and all the pleasures of our senses are the only law to be satisfied. Serve yourselves my brothers, in the name of prince our lord, and honour Thule..."* The Commander put his money where his mouth was and raised his sash, revealing an erect cock. **He approaches a little girl of around twelve who has been sobbing since the start of the ceremony. The child is barely resisting (...) Already, men and women have stepped aside to give themselves over to their pleasure, others are grabbing children... Samir feels himself being palpated, turned inside out... then sinks into a kind of waking coma, a total insensitivity, as if all this were not true, as if his body were not his body, as if he were just an observer**

of this odious meeting..." (**Samir enters a state of total insensitivity here, as if his body were not his body, as if he were just an observer of this odious meeting...**"). (Samir enters a dissociative state here)

This is a "**paedo-satanic**" ritual involving the rape and torture of children under cover of a Luciferian doctrine summed up as "***Do what you will is the whole of the law***". The "Alliance Kripten" sect practising these horrors seems to apply to the letter the rituals of the Golden Dawn, itself derived from the Masonic spheres... As mentioned at the beginning of this document, this is an initiatory *Russian doll* in which various *esoteric schools* overlap, some opening doors to others in a highly selective initiation process. **We are not talking about "*Masonic deviations*" or**

"marginal deviant groups", we are talking about the most profound - and most elitist - sects of Masonic essence, where Good and Evil no longer exist...

In the Alègre case, the confessions of a judge seem to confirm the existence of these ultra-violent sectarian groups practising ritual crimes in France... Pierre Roche, at the time president of the Montpellier Court of Appeal, died in 2003 in a suspicious manner. His children, **Charles-Louis Roche** and his sister **Diane**, both lawyers, claim that their father was a victim of the network in which he himself was involved. A few weeks before his death, feeling threatened and under pressure, the judge confided in them, recounting his "turpitudes" in a form of repentance and extreme guilt. He described the criminal rituals of this sectarian group... In 2005, Charles-Louis Roche publicly denounced his father's macabre confidences: "**It was very clear, our father told us about a kind of sect behind which there was a kind of ideological corpus...**

Charles-Louis Roche

How does this sect work? People with power are approached; if you don't have power, you're not interesting. So as soon as someone has power, they can be of use and we might consider recruiting them, as long as we have detected the moral corruption in them that will make them a suitable member. Above all, you don't want to recruit someone who could break up the group or who could denounce what they have witnessed. So we recruit people who seem interesting and in whom **we have detected this sort of vocation, which I would describe as diabolical... We start by inviting this person to parties that are less extreme**

than those they will later attend, but during which we lock them up by filming what happens during these parties. This ensures the member's future loyalty and that they will never talk to anyone. Then we move on to more and more serious things... The morality, if I may say so, or the ideology behind this group, is very serious in terms of what it reveals about our society...

In this group, they are told that all the rules that have been put in their heads since the beginning, whether at school, in society, etc., are limitations on their freedom, preventing them from reaching the *quintessence of the human race*, and that they must therefore reject all rules, starting with laws, morals and decency. There is a need to transgress these rules, to violate, sometimes literally, all the taboos in order to break through the sort of locks that have been placed in our heads since childhood. That's how you start with rape and torture, and end up with murder... So here are people who, after that, become completely unbridled, imbued with their powers, and who are led, by encouraging each other, to go ever further in horror (...)

Our father told us about people from the medical world, even from universities. This secret group recruited a lot of people from legal circles, and even high-ranking police officers were highly regarded. So this was a secret group whose activities consisted of conducting ceremonies of some kind in the greatest secrecy, combining practices as strange and uniformly disgusting as group sex and scarification? He conjured up images that would make your hair stand on end. He spoke of charred flesh, cigarette burns, pierced flesh. He told us that people were tortured, **sometimes even killed during these sessions...** There were sick people who demanded this kind of treatment, but there were also **non-consenting people, sometimes children, who were first tortured, then put to death, the whole thing filmed and the subject of a traffic in illegal videos that would be traded under the cloak at crazy prices.** He told us that the prey of this group of high-society predators were recruited from the lowest strata of society, from the categories of people who would never be wanted. He spoke of prostitutes, he spoke of "*tramps*", and I quote the term used by a magistrate. Sometimes he even mentioned illegal aliens, depending on what they could get their hands on, I imagine. In other words, people who have either severed their links with their environment or have no legal existence, people who no one is going to go looking for or about whom any investigation will be more or less doomed to failure from the outset. **Of course, the members of this group, because of the influential positions they occupy, are in a position, if certain cases threaten to come to light, to nip in the bud by manipulating the levers at their disposal, especially as they all have each other by the scruff of the neck...".**

In 2008, Charles-Louis Roche gave a series of free lectures at the Théâtre de la Main d'Or in Paris. In them, the lawyer described the backstage workings of our institutions, based on revelations made by his father. Could Patrice Alègre, whom the media portrayed as a lone serial killer, have been nothing more than a supplier of 'fresh meat' for *the Brotherhood* network in the Toulouse region?

"Do you want to know what's behind all the cases we've heard so much about in recent years? Alègre, Dutroux, Fourniret, the Yonne disappearances, and all the others we never hear about... well, they all follow the same pattern (...) The *serial killer* is a very convenient explanation, he's the perfect whistle-blower. He's the madman who did it all! Why is that? Because he's a madman, move along, there's nothing to see, look no further. Above all, don't try to trace it back to our Masters, who are the masterminds behind the Alègre, Fourniret and consorts, who are merely the fiftieth-zone executors, suppliers of fresh meat for their evenings in hell! **What lies behind this affair is the political protection afforded to paedophiles and kidnappers, right up to the highest levels of government. A list of seventy-one paedophile judges, kept secret by the Chancellery, continues to enjoy this protection to this day. Seventy-one paedophile judges, covered up and still in office! I would even go so far as to say that they are all the more covered up and** still in office because they have become so useful! Now that we have a file on them and they're in an ejector seat, they'll do exactly what those in power tell them to do.

Psychosociologist and writer **Christian Cotten** met the children of Judge Pierre Roche on several occasions. Charles-Louis and Diane told him in detail about their father's statements on this sectarian group in the Toulouse region; statements that Cotten had already heard from certain police officers:

"What, in a nutshell, are they talking about? They're talking about what some might call "satanic practices"... It seems that their father told them that he had taken part in **ritual, organised, structured ceremonies conducted by what Charles-Louis calls "celebrants".** So we're dealing with something **approaching 'religious' practices,** where people seem to come

together to have a collective experience with practices of group sexuality (...) The problem starts when they start telling us about torture, various abuses practised on the participants, and then especially when they start telling us that a certain number of these ceremonies end in death (...).) We're not talking here about people who might be thought to be suffering from various and sundry psychiatric pathologies... no, we're talking about judges, politicians, financiers, academics, media men... **In other words, notables who come together through mutual sponsorship from generation to generation. I remember hearing the same thing from retired police officers who told me exactly the same stories, explaining that a certain number of politicians were bound by this type of mafia system through collective sexual practices ending in ritual murders...** And unfortunately, I recognise in Charles-Louis and Diane's testimonies exactly what these police officers told me. What really disturbs me about

Charles and Diane's testimony is that it seems to be totally linked to the Allègre affair, since the socio-professional environment of their father, Mr Pierre Roche. We find the same names, the same magistrates (...) Need we remind you that the Alègre affair in Toulouse involved 190 unsolved murders over a period of ten years, many of which were disguised as fake suicides by the same 'experts' (forensic doctors), who we can legitimately wonder if they might not have been part of the group to which Pierre Roche claims to have belonged (...).) How is it possible that in what we call a democratic republic, a state governed by the rule of law, institutional systems can lead to this kind of practice... I don't really have the answer to that question, I just wonder...".

It is in the Great Mysteries of contemporary secret societies that we find the explanations for these ritualised, criminal, extreme and irrational practices...

Former Toulouse police captain Alain Vidal, who conducted a parallel investigation into the Alègre affair, reported: "These evenings took place in around Toulouse and even in establishments in neighbouring departments. It goes without saying that it wasn't just anyone who met in such places, but relatively well-off people such as **company directors (public works, construction, car dealers, lawyers, politicians, elected**

representatives, doctors, notables from all walks of life, etc). One of them, who was particularly violent, used to disguise himself as a monk to satisfy his fantasies... **I'm not forgetting some of my former colleagues, or gendarmes, who were undoubtedly less well-off, but who were able to provide a few small services...**

According to one hostess, there were sometimes as many as seventy people per evening, preferably wearing masks (but in the dark, the masks fell off by themselves), so that all the "beau monde" could recognise each other. It was even reported that each participant paid the sum of 4,000 francs.

Another para-Masonic Gnostic group that has been accused of **paedo-satanic** practices **and ritual crimes** is **Martinism**, mentioned at the beginning of this document. The Martinist doctrine, established in particular by Martinès de Pasqually, is a "Christian" esotericism described as illuminist. **Martinism is one of the mystical and spiritual branches of Freemasonry.** As these two orders have common foundations and a large number of mutual affiliations of their members, we can say that they are intertwined: initiation in a Masonic lodge is generally the first step before access to esoteric schools such as Martinism.

Société

Eux aussi, ils prostituaient leurs enfants

Un couple et une femme appartenant au réseau pédophile d'Angers viennent d'être arrêtés. L'enquête s'intéresse à d'autres milieux.

Véronique Liaigre is one of the victims of the Angers paedophile ring, a case that hit the headlines in 2001. **Véronique told investigators that her parents "rented" her out to wealthy people... She also claimed to have taken part in satanic ritual abuse within a Martinist group...**

On 5 July 2001, TF1 broadcast a report on this survivor. Here are some extracts:

Off voice: Véronique is 20 years old and has lived through hell since the age of 5. Raped and prostituted by her parents, whom she denounced and who are waiting to appear before the Assize Court, she has managed to escape from those she calls her executioners. Her story is not an ordinary one, and may even seem invented. However, while it is legitimate to have doubts, what this young woman told us and repeated spontaneously is shocking. **Particularly when she claims, despite the threats she says were made against her, to have frequented a Satanist sect, the Martinists, and to have been tortured and tortured herself.**

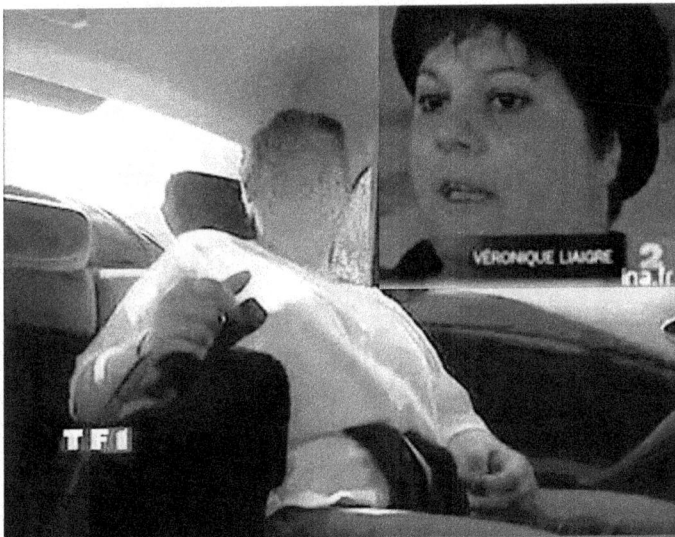

- Véronique Liaigre: **We are beaten, we have objects put in our orifices, sometimes children are sacrificed to give thanks to Satan, there are many things like that...** They kill an animal, pour the blood over its head and put the rest in a dome on the altar.

- Journalist: So in fact, your parents, like all the parents of these children you're talking about, sold their children?

- VL: Exactly, because it brings in a certain percentage of money. **A child under the age of 8 is worth 22,000 francs.**

- J : Where do these children come from?

- VL : **The children who are sacrificed are not declared, or are foreign children.** Particularly when I was in Agen, they were little Africans, they were black. I saw them in Jallais too, and in Nanterre too, but they were white children, French children, **but they were children born of rape (...) that hadn't been declared. They were given birth in their parents' homes in appalling conditions (...)**

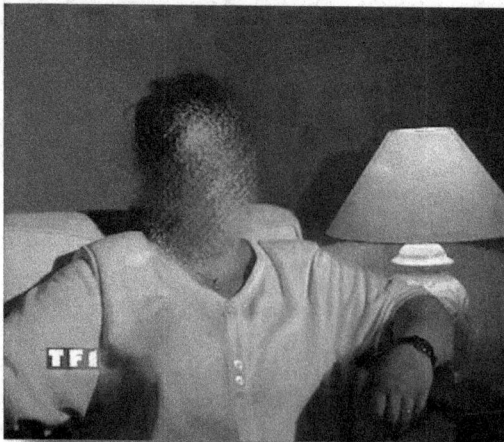

- J: Not only were you part of the sect, but you also took part in these rituals...

- VL: Yes. In 1994, **two of my friends and I had to sacrifice a child in Jallais at gunpoint.** And the three of us had to kill him... at gunpoint, because if we didn't, we would have been... they would have done it even more violently and they would have hurt us even more. So we had to do it...

- J: And who was pointing a gun at you?

- VL: "bleep" **for the man in charge of the** "bleep" **gendarmerie** (...)

- J : You think that all this is a kind of network, people holding on to each other a little so as not to fall...

- VL: That's it, and it's also to protect ourselves, **because given that there are lawyers involved, it's true that it would make a bit of a fuss if people found out that there were judges and so on who were part of this network.**

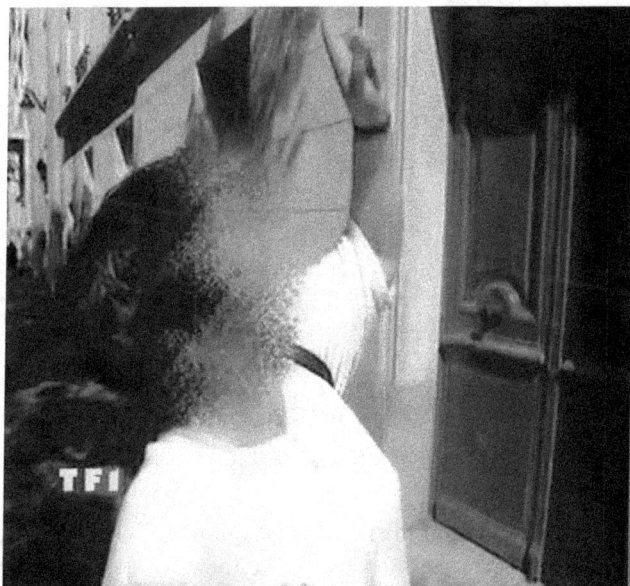

- Voice-over: **Véronique took us to one of the many places where, according to her, satanic ceremonies took place on the 21st of each month.**

- VL (at the foot of a city centre building in front of a porte cochère): I've been here several times. I remember well one time in 1994, when **I was at a satanic ritual involving the murder of a child.** We went up to the second floor. **There were rapes, there must have been 5 or 6 children, it wasn't a very big meeting.** There were "beeps" and "beeps", **there were a lot of people, including some notables whose names I don't necessarily know.**

- J: And you yourself have been through...

 - VL: **Yes, I was there and I suffered... My father was there, but my mother wasn't that time.**

To conclude this chapter devoted to testimonies, here is an extract from the dossier "*Le protocole des ignobles en robes noires*" (*The protocol of the despicable in black robes)* written by former gendarme **Christian Maillaud**, alias **Stan Maillaud**, who has been working on paedocriminal networks for over fifteen years. The man is now, in 2020, wrongfully incarcerated by a judicial system that has run out of steam...

The reproduction of paedophile criminals, generation after generation

There is a phenomenon that the "general public" does not know about, and which forms the backdrop to the issues we are dealing with in this dossier. **It is the process of "initiation into paedophilia" undergone by countless children in France and**

around the world. As you will see, this concept alone explains the chronic *dysfunction* of our judicial institution.

It is in the context of "special evenings" that the child of a "notable" most certainly undergoes a formal process of "initiation into paedophilia". There are many accounts of children being taken by their own parents to "turn up" at these special evenings, where they are regularly gang raped and tortured. In the majority of cases, the parent who inflicts these horrors on his own child is a man, but there are a few cases where it may also be the couple, or just the mother. It's hard to imagine a woman sexually abusing children, but that doesn't mean it doesn't happen. Depending on the extent and duration of the treatment, the programming applied to children through violence is also applied to young girls, who then also become predators when they reach adulthood (...)

The mentally ill who belong to the "elite" circles are therefore invited to bring their own children to the sessions to "prepare" them to become the submissive predators that the network wants to turn them into, to the great glory of their progenitors. So, depending on the "importance", the lodge and the rank of the "notables" in question, these children may even undergo initiation into the sacrificial murder that their own progenitors most likely went through themselves as children, making them what they are today. In this case, the unfortunate children are

destined to officiate at a level far above the average, probably at the political level (...) To understand the scale of the problem in 'our' society, it is essential to consider that a victim who is not rescued most often becomes an executioner in his or her own right.

The suffering experienced in the early years, both physical and psychological, can only be tolerated over the long term if the subject ends up adhering to the treatment inflicted on him or her (in the very short term, the mere concealment of reality may suffice, although the repercussions in terms of personality disorders may not be too serious).

This suffering, never treated, of a child martyred over the long term and never rescued, will then be buried in the subconscious, with the message that playing the torturer's game was the only way to survive his monstrosities. At this point, the 'subject' will have been invited to switch from the role of victim to that of executioner, coming to the unspeakable realisation that this was the only way to stop being a victim.

This process is also reminiscent of Stockholm syndrome, where the hostage ends up siding with the hostage-taker and adhering to his cause, following the trauma he undergoes, between terror and powerlessness. The notion of injustice, for its part, enters into the subconscious of the "subject" as a major frustration, never consciously acknowledged, and therefore never dealt with. This notion will never have been made conscious because the 'subject' will have been led to bury it in his subconscious, also hiding this notion of injustice and favouring the only way out, which was to become an executioner himself. Let's not forget that to bear the unbearable, the human brain activates a process of denial and concealment of the real experience, which leads to the splitting of the personality. It's very easy for well-informed torturers, like the common victim-breakers of "classic" pimping networks, to reach the threshold of what their prey can bear, to the point where the prey naturally triggers the psychological "survival" process that turns them into slaves incapable of the slightest rebellion.

But the suffering is still there, deeply buried in the subconscious of every broken victim. This suffering and these feelings will pervade them for the rest of their lives. To mop up this suffering and its unconscious frustrations, the 'subject' will have been led, encouraged by his torturers over the years, to develop mechanisms that are basically already natural, of transferring onto other vulnerable subjects. This original "subject", now an adult, in the absence of in-depth therapy, therefore continues to deal with his own suffering through sexual aggression, which he most often reproduces on his own children.

For if the ex-victim was herself abused as a child by her own parents, her own offspring is precisely what enables her to make this transference, this form of 'exorcising' the suffering she has experienced. These psychic processes have been extensively studied and decoded for ages by those who wish to control humanity. At the same time, the brainwashing and mental manipulation applied in meetings of secret societies such as Freemasonry, at certain levels, spread the belief that the practice of this type of "sexual magic", applied even to one's own children, is what enables the initiate to exalt his potential for domination, while preparing future generations - his progeny - to follow this path of "chosen one".

This unfortunate offspring is thus programmed to become tomorrow's elite, perfectly psychologically deranged, a veritable 'Dr Jekyll and Mr Hyde'.

This enables the notables concerned, the paedophile criminals of the pseudo-elite and their networks of influence, to reassure the general public, who have been manipulated into believing that there is no paedophile network other than isolated criminals, monstrous specimens from the "lower classes". But, if the problem can be avoided - or if it is not in fact a communication campaign organised by the political and judicial sham - the criminal in question will willingly be protected by what appears to be the armed wing of the network: the judiciary!

There is another pattern that is very widespread today: the criminal you, as a protective parent, may be dealing with belongs to circles of influence such as Rosicrucianism or Freemasonry, from which he derives his impunity. Behind secret societies of this type, we find a whole process of co-optation and ritual initiation, which gradually and formally drifts towards Satanism. Beyond the eighteenth degree in Freemasonry, the rituals become increasingly odious, going as far as child sacrifice.

Obviously, the vast majority of people co-opted into these secret societies have no initial doubt that organised crime and Satanism are involved. It is presented to them as just the opposite, and, at the height of Machiavellianism, there is talk of philanthropy and charity. It is only by climbing the ladder, over time, that a Freemason will realise what he really belongs to. In the meantime, he will have been deeply compromised, and will have tasted the poisoned fruits of debauchery and power, of unpunished crime, of that exclusive feeling of being above the law and the "uncultured and stupid masses" (...) before reaching that point, members are insidiously directed towards group sexual practices, the orgies so "trendy" and openly applauded by the political sham that speaks to us of "liberalism". Orgies have become the preferred form of entertainment for the "notables". Beyond the "joyful evening", the subjects involved are imperceptibly sliding towards sexual magic, which is highly prized in Satanism.

For those who, naively, thought they were just having fun with friends from the 'upper crust', at a given moment, everything changes. For the well-informed initiates at these joyous parties, the expression of their power is all the more exalted as innocent pre-pubescent victims suffer the effects of their impulses, with the perfect impunity reserved for them by their status... The rape of the pure and innocent, with its sacrifice, is the constant expression of domination of others, as well as an essential support for satanic ritual. The more heinous the crime, the greater the sense of impunity that attaches to it, giving the perpetrator a feeling of supreme power, and, if necessary, a little cocaine removes any ability to pull oneself together.

If everyone is holding on to each other's... whiskers, in this type of private circle, a taste for unhealthy power over others and debauchery quickly develops in severely compromised members. They choose to see only the 'good side' of the situation, plunging body and soul into the abyss into which they are plunged as they pass through the ranks and undergo initiation rituals. The pseudo-elites concerned, depending on their lodge and rank, come to appreciate private parties where children are collectively raped, some even tortured, sometimes to the point of sacrificial death (...) **Our ongoing investigation into this extension of the present subject is currently attempting to prove that these practices are widespread throughout France, following the example of Belgium, just like Satanism, and always, it should be pointed out, at the level of the so-called circles of power...**

The emblem of the Scottish Rite perfectly represents this notion of duality, of dual personality, through the representation of a two-headed eagle...

L'aigle à deux têtes, emblème du Rite Écossais Ancien et Accepté, figure sur cette bannière de l'orient de Valenciennes.

Just like Janus, the ancient Roman god with two faces, dear to Freemasons...

The Widow's Sons and Schizophrenia

Psychiatry, and schizophrenia in particular, seems to be of great interest to the *Widow's Sons*...

In 1934, in the United States, the Scottish Rite of Freemasonry joined the Rockefeller Foundation in funding genetic psychiatry and inaugurated a research programme on schizophrenia. Since the *Scottish Rite Schizophrenia Research Program (SRSRP)* was set up as a charitable foundation, funding has continued to increase thanks to contributions from members of the Masonic fraternity. Since 1934, over 6 million dollars have been allocated

to this research programme on schizophrenia. The official aim of the programme is to advance understanding of the nature and causes of schizophrenia... The SRSRP was based at St Elizabeth's Hospital, Washington DC, at the time, under the leadership of Dr Winfred Overholser, a Freemason and leading member of the American Psychiatric Association and linked to the US Army's mind control experiments. St Elizabeth's Hospital was later known to have housed CIA mind control experiments (MK-Ultra).

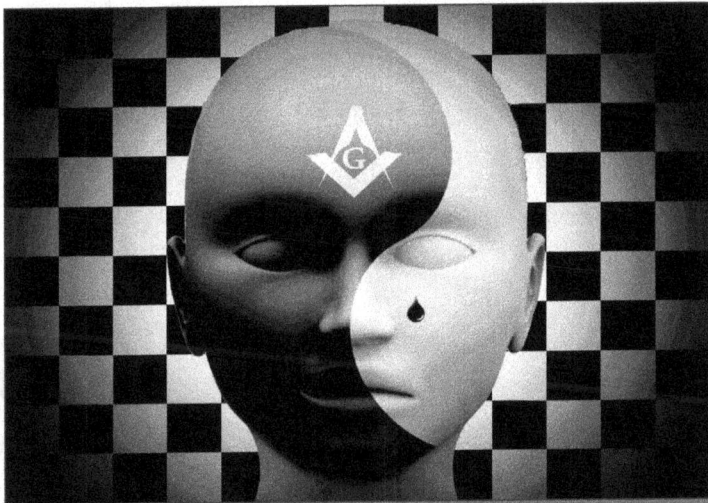

Freemasonry's donations for the study of these mental disorders were allocated for clearly defined projects (orientation), rather than for overall support for research. One such project was to fund the eugenicist psychiatrist Franz J. Kallmann to conduct a study of 1,000 cases of schizophrenia, with the aim of highlighting the hereditary factor in this disorder. Kallmann's

155 |

study was published simultaneously in the United States and Nazi Germany in 1938. Even today, certain specialists such as Dr. Kenneth Kendler (who has also received financial support from the Scottish Rite/SRSRP) publish studies claiming that schizophrenia is genetic in origin, thus ruling out the question of dissociative disorders and traumatic origins.

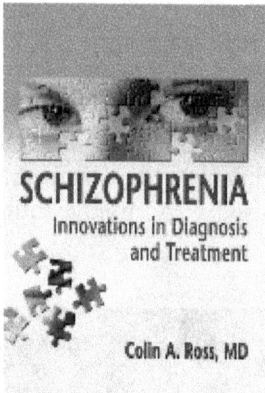

SCHIZOPHRENIA
Innovations in Diagnosis and Treatment

Colin A. Ross, MD

Dr Colin Ross refutes the purely genetic origin and denounces the dishonesty of these so-called "scientific" studies. A specialist in dissociative disorders, Colin Ross claims that many patients suffering from "schizophrenia" present symptoms closely linked to dissociative identity disorder. Patients who also have a history of psychological trauma. Asserting that schizophrenia has a mainly genetic cause rules out any environmental cause, particularly severe trauma in early childhood...

Schizophrenia is now a kind of catch-all drawer masking the reality of dissociative identity disorder. The following symptoms are very often misdiagnosed as *schizophrenia*: dissociative amnesia, depersonalisation, the presence of several distinct personalities/identities, auditory hallucinations, etc.

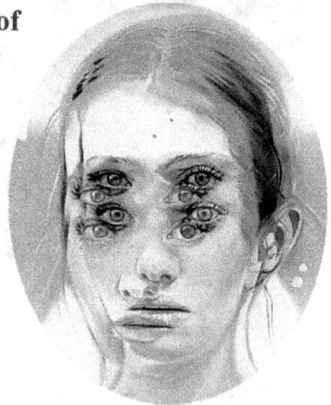

With regard to "auditory hallucinations" or "voices in the head" - which is a symptom systematically considered to be "schizophrenia" - it may be a case of split personality (I.D.T.) and internal dialogue with alter personalities. In the 1994 edition of the DSM, the symptoms of voices that talk to each other or systematically comment on the person's behaviour were considered to be "schizophrenic". Many psychotherapists working with patients with IDD have found that the phenomenon of 'voices in the head' is common in people with a long history of trauma. More and more studies seem to be making the link between dissociation and these "auditory hallucinations". Some studies have focused exclusively on this issue, such as Charlotte Connor and Max Birchwood's *"Abuse and dysfunctional affiliations in childhood: An exploration of their impact on voice-hearer's appraisals of power and expressed emotion"*, or Vasiliki Fenekou and Eugenie Georgaca's *"Exploring the experience of hearing voices: A qualitative study"*.

To illustrate the link between *'voices in the head'*, IDD and trauma, let's go back to the testimony of the multiple Régina Louf (Dutroux case): *"It had always been like that. In Knokke, at my grandmother's house, **the adults noticed that I spoke to the voices in my head, that I changed moods quickly, or even that I started to speak with a different voice or accent.** Although I was only 5 or 6 years old, I understood that something like that was bizarre and not allowed. **I learned to hide my voices, my other selves.** After what had happened to Clo, the voices, and the strange feeling that I was sometimes led by inner voices became stronger. After the initiation, I could no longer resist the voices. **I was happy to disappear into nothingness**, only to regain consciousness when Tony was there. The pain seemed more bearable.*

At a phenomenological level, there is a significant overlap between the symptoms of dissociative disorders (particularly I.D.D.) and schizophrenia. **One study showed that a group of patients diagnosed with schizophrenia by a psychiatrist or psychologist, to whom you give a standardised interview relating to dissociative symptoms, showed that 35 to 40% of these patients, who were supposed to be schizophrenic, came away with a diagnosis of dissociative identity disorder. Conversely, in a group of patients diagnosed with D.I.D. to whom you give an interview linked to schizophrenic symptoms, two thirds will emerge with a diagnosis of schizophrenia.**

A group of 236 I.D.D. patients showed that 40.8% had previously been diagnosed with schizophrenia (*"Multiple personality disorder patients with a prior diagnosis of schizophrenia"* - Colin Ross, G. Ron Norton, Journal "Dissociation", Vol.1 N°2, 06/1988).

In a study entitled *"Dissociation and Schizophrenia"* published in 2004 in the journal *Trauma and Dissociation*, Dr Colin Ross and Dr Benjamin Keyes assessed dissociative symptoms in a group of 60 individuals being treated for schizophrenia. They found that 36 subjects showed significant dissociative features, i.e. 60% of their sample. These dissociative symptoms were accompanied by a high rate of childhood trauma, as well as major disorders such as depression, *Borderline* Personality Disorder and I.D.D..

Whether in the case of I.D.D. or schizophrenia, dissociation is an underlying feature, as is the traumatic origin of these personality disorders.

Despite studies that have clearly shown the link between psychotic disorders, dissociative disorders and trauma, there has been a sharp decline in the use of the diagnosis of dissociative disorders. **This decline can be explained in particular by the introduction of the term "*Schizophrenia*" to describe patients showing this type of symptom.** Between 1911 and 1927, the number of reported cases of multiple personality disorder, now known as dissociative identity disorder, fell by almost half following the replacement of the term "*Dementia Preacox*" by "*Schizophrenia*" by the Swiss psychiatrist Eugen Bleuler.

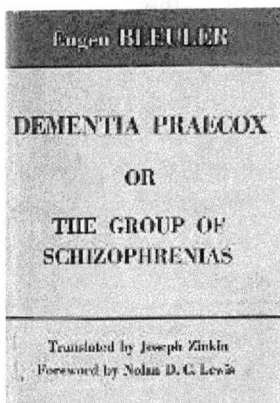

Dr. Rosenbaum explains this in detail in his article "*The role of the term* **schizophrenia** *in the decline of* **diagnoses** *of multiple personality*".

Fritz Springmeier maintains that tens of thousands of individuals hospitalised in psychiatric wards for '*schizophrenia*' are multiple programmers: victims who have developed I.D.D. as a result of trauma-based mind control protocols. To describe these individuals (the *broken butterflies*) as *"paranoid schizophrenics"* is to undermine their credibility. This would make it possible to get rid of them discreetly by burying them in the electroshock and chemistry of psychiatric institutes.

In cases of paedo-crime networks where the victims are highly dissociated by extreme trauma, we find that very often their word is discredited because of their mental health... This is a crucial point on which the perpetrators rely to dismiss disturbing testimony: the victims are obviously dissociated by repetitive trauma and this "faulty" psychological state is therefore highlighted in order to nullify their testimony... This is an unhealthy inversion that ignores the phenomenon of cause and effect: **a witness suffering from severe dissociative disorders must have experienced trauma...**

This is where information control comes in, i.e. making sure that research into dissociative disorders gets out into the public domain as little as possible. Everything possible has been done to avoid linking dissociative disorders to trauma, apart from simply ignoring the reality of the phenomenon of dissociation and its psychological consequences... to replace it with a catch-all, anxiety-provoking term:

SCHIZOPHRENIA.

For over 80 years, Freemasonry has invested millions in research into *'Dementia Preacox'*, or *'Schizophrenia'*, which as we have just seen is very often caused by severe dissociative disorders resulting from trauma - and what are the therapeutic results? - Today, patients diagnosed with 'schizophrenia' are heavily chemically medicated for the benefit of pharmaceutical laboratories.

One of the negative consequences of these misdiagnoses is that the treatment given for 'schizophrenia' will be based mainly on heavy, addictive and even dangerous medication... Whereas in I.D.D. therapy, treatment with medication is something secondary; chemistry can be used to treat co-morbidity but it is not therapeutic in the strict sense of the word. **The psychiatric establishment seems to have little desire to really help victims and survivors of trauma, neglecting or completely ignoring the subject of psycho-traumatology and dissociative phenomena.**

The decision-making power of the Masonic High Lodges has nothing to do with the well-being of "schizophrenics"... On the other hand, when we realise that "schizophrenia" is linked in many ways to multiple personality disorder or dissociative identity disorder, or even demonic possession, which most survivors of ritual abuse and mind control suffer from, we begin to understand the interest of the Masonic lobby in investing in this field in order to control and direct research in this area... particularly that which rules out the diagnosis of I.D.D. in favour of a "catch-all schizophrenia".I.D.D. diagnosis in favour of a "catch-all schizophrenia" and any traumatic origin in favour of a purely genetic origin. What's more, a victim dissociated by traumatic rituals and subsequently wrongly diagnosed as "schizophrenic" will have his or her words rejected and reduced to nothing, because they are considered to be *psychotic delirium* (a godsend for the aggressors)... Whereas the dissociative disorders from which he or she suffers should, on the contrary, be a strong indicator of his or her traumatic experience and the importance of his or her story.

Kathleen Sullivan, a survivor of ritual abuse who developed dissociative identity disorder, writes in her autobiography: "*I felt despair when I remembered what Grandad always said to me before leaving me alone in that room: that no one would believe me if I spoke, because the doctor had written in my file that I was schizophrenic. Grandad often reminded me that "nobody believes schizophrenics, everyone knows they're mad*". (*Unshackled: a survivor's story of mind control* - Kathleen Sullivan, 2003)

So there is a communication war, or rather a "*Memory War*", when it comes to scientific research into how the brain works in the face of trauma. As a result, misinformation and a withholding of information are being put in place to prevent these studies from being widely disseminated and taught in medical faculties, which could have a major impact in the courts to defend the - disassociated - victims of these paedocriminal networks...

The Pandora's box of ritual abuse and trauma-based mind control, i.e. the neurological process of dissociation and traumatic amnesia, is covered by a blanket of secrecy. Teaching the scientific workings of dissociation, amnesic walls and personality splitting in medical faculties would be tantamount to publicly and academically revealing knowledge belonging to the deepest occultism (knowledge reserved for the high initiates of secret societies). This knowledge, however, is ancestral and is used today in a systematic and malicious way by certain power groups. The process by which slaves function under mental programming is not supposed to reach the public and profane sphere...

Most students of psychology and psychiatry do not believe that such mind control is possible. This is for the good reason that they have no knowledge of the basic concept behind trauma-based mind control, i.e. M.P.D., a multiple personality disorder with amnesia, which is essential if a human is to work like a robot in clandestine operations... or not.

"To date, neither the American Psychiatric Association nor the American Psychological Association has published a model for the development of an effective therapeutic protocol for dissociative disorders (considered to be the result of repeated traumas). A number of factors make the development of such a model difficult. The first of these factors concerns the secrecy that National Security applies to classified mind control research. In the current climate, referring victims of mind control to psychiatric professionals for treatment would be like referring a patient in need of emergency surgery to a surgeon who has been blindfolded and handcuffed (...) What might allow us to lay the foundations of an explanation would be to identify 'who? "If you take the next step and pick up a copy of the faculty

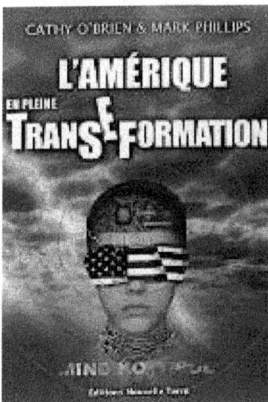

professor's *Oxford's Companion To The Mind* (Oxford Press, 1987), you can find almost everything about mind research without the slightest reference to mind control. Perhaps now you will be able to see through the omissions of Random House, Webster and other Oxford <u>Press</u>, <u>that you are a victim of information control."</u>

("L'Amérique en pleine transe-formation" - Cathy O'Brien & Mark Phillips - Éditions Nouvelle Terre, 2013, p.62-19)

Conclusion

This dossier on Freemasonry and Schizophrenia raises some legitimate and disturbing questions. Firstly, about the distant origins of Freemasonry, which, according to some writings of high FM degrees, can be traced back to the ancient Mystery religions. As we have seen, the pagan practices of some of these Mystery religions included traumatic initiation rituals, but also a certain fertility cult involving orgiastic practices, blood sacrifices and even blood baptism in the cult of Mithras, which is similar in many respects to modern Freemasonry. This is a starting point for understanding some of the accounts given by victims and survivors of ritual abuse, because at first sight these accounts may seem fanciful and invented.

All these alleged victims describe having undergone the same traumatic ritual practices aimed at achieving dissociative states for the purpose of mental control...

We note that Freemasonry is a common factor in many of these testimonies... What interest would these survivors, scattered all over the world, have in specifying that their attackers were Freemasons? How is it that the same methods of torture and mental programming are described by victims who have never met before? How can such things be invented?

We note that the American Jeanette Westbrook - daughter of a high-ranking Freemason - describes exactly the same mind control protocol as witness X1 in the **Dutroux** case, Régina Louf: **i.e. the cultivation and maintenance of dissociative identity disorder (and its amnesic walls), resulting from incest and torture, for the purposes of mind control and sexual exploitation.** This is also what was described by American survivor Cathy O'Brien, author of the book "*America in the midst of Transformation*", who was sexually enslaved in high political circles because of her dissociative identity disorder caused by paternal incest.

We note that Samir Aouchiche's testimony concerning a pedo-satanic ceremony of the crypto-Masonic Golden Dawn is totally in line with the testimony of Judge Pierre Roche concerning the "philosophical" motivations of these pedocriminal sects:

Aouchiche reports the words of the master of ceremonies: *"Through our sexuality, freed at last from the yoke of our Judeo-Christian oppressors, we purify ourselves (...) Sex and all the pleasures of our senses are the only law to be satisfied".*

This corresponds perfectly to what Charles-Louis Roche says about the secret society to which his father belonged: *"In this group, they are told that all the rules that have been put in their heads since the beginning, whether at school, in society, etc., are limitations on their freedom, preventing them from reaching the quintessence of the human race, and that they must therefore reject all rules, starting with laws, morals and decency. There is a need to transgress these rules, to violate, sometimes literally, all the taboos in order to break through the sort of locks that have been placed in our heads since childhood. That's how we start with rape and torture, and end up with murder...".*

As we have seen, these secret societies operate with a system of duality, or plurality, serving to conceal their profound nature... On the one hand from all laymen, but also and above all to hide their highly immoral, even criminal, practices from the seduced and freshly initiated souls - in *fraternal joviality*. The adept must therefore be gradually shaped and transformed in the manner of *modelling clay*. **It's a process of** *"spiritual scouring"* **designed to break down all moral barriers one by one**. This gradual 'scouring' is necessary to break down the *taboos* that stand in the way of the quest for *knowledge and spiritual awakening*. As the initiation progresses, the adept is gradually cut off from his or her true moral compass. **This is how an absolute relativism is established, eventually eliminating any notion of Good or Evil**. Subtle veils and multiple doctrinal and intellectual mystifications must therefore be used to hide the "holy of holies" from those who are not yet able to integrate the *final message* of this "revelation". This morbid (or counter-initiatory) process is greatly simplified when the individual is already a member of the "Family"; he or she will then have been subjected from earliest childhood to extreme traumatic protocols aimed on the one hand at developing the dissociative states necessary for mental programming and on the other at suppressing any notion of compassion that might hinder his or her rise in society. In the upper echelons of secret societies, the splitting up of children's personalities through traumatic *initiation* rituals is systematic. Whether mafia, religious, political or military groups (all under the umbrella of initiation brotherhoods), in a general and international way, they all know that dissociation, the fragmentation of the personality, is the key to secrecy and power; but also a key to obtaining certain hyper-creative individuals with very high intelligence quotients.

It's a vicious circle for these individuals, who were put through the *psychic mill* in their early childhood, because if they don't extricate themselves from these spheres of influence they will reproduce these patterns in their own descendants, who are subject to the Lodge. It's a veritable vicious circle for families mired in occultism and dissociative states. That's why it's imperative to expose these practices to the light of the *profane world*, in order to cut the evil at its roots and prevent it from developing.

This destructive philosophy of achieving **"redemption through sin"**, or **"holiness through evil"**, is aimed at **the systematic inversion of moral values, where evil becomes good and good becomes evil**. In his book entitled *"Le Messie Militant"*, Arthur Mandel defines this notion of "redemption through sin" as follows: *"It is nothing other than the old Pauline-Gnostic idea of felix culpa, the holy sin of the road to God passing through sin, the perverse desire to fight evil with evil, to get rid of sin by sinning"*.

This obscure doctrine is propagated largely by the infiltration and subversion of religions, but also of

institutions working behind the scenes of governments and behind democratic facades.

Australian criminologist Michael Salter, author of the book *"Organised Sexual Abuse"*, describes these notions of systematic infiltration and inversion as follows: *"**Survivors have described how these families and groups practising ritual abuse overlap with religious institutions or fraternal organisations** (...) **In their ritual abuse practices, these people seem to adopt and invert the traditional rituals of the large organisations they have infiltrated. Survivors describe living in 'two worlds' as children: benevolent religious and fraternal institutions and ideologies on the one hand, entangled with deviant and sadistic rituals on the other"*. ("The Role of Ritual in the Organised Abuse of Children", 2012 - Michael Salter)

When it comes to infiltration and double-dealing, there is **Frankism** and **Sabbataoism**, a satanic degeneration of Judaism and the Kabbalah, founded by the self-proclaimed 'Messiahs' Sabbatai Tsevi (17th century) and Jacob Frank (18th century). *Sabbatao-Frankism* can be considered a close ancestor of the Bavarian Illuminati, among others... Strictly speaking, there is no Frankist or Sabbataist cult, since it is a clandestine doctrine and philosophy propagated by infiltration and subversion.

In his book *"Jacob Frank, the False Messiah"*, Charles Novak writes about Frankism: *"So while Judaism preaches virginity, fidelity and love, Sabbataï and his successors like Jacob Frank preach sex from an early age for young girls, sexual orgies for young boys and wife swapping on Shabbat. To the extent that some Frankist children do not know their real biological father. In January 1756, Jacob and his followers were caught in the middle of an orgiastic Shabbat in the town of Landskron and, at the request of the rabbis, were expelled from the town for orgies. A woman stood naked in the middle while the male followers chanted the Jewish Shabbat prayer (...) Then they pounced on her, turning the ritual into a collective orgy. The Frankist sexual rites then consisted of songs, ecstatic dances, mixing men and women (...) the men and women would undress and the collective orgy would begin, the nudity reminiscent of Adam and Eve before the fall (...) The Frankists were known for their sometimes violent collective sexual orgies.* This nihilistic behaviour, in which the 9th of April became a festival of joy, led to the exchange of women, **where the aim was to destroy all dogma...**

Here we find the sacred orgies practised in the ancient religions known as the 'Mysteries', such as the cult of Dionysus/Bacchus, the phallic cult linked to fertility, just like the Shivaïc cult in India or the cult of Osiris in ancient Egypt with its obelisks symbolising the phallus.

It is legitimate to think that such horrors, practised on such a large scale, cannot remain sheltered from journalists, police investigations and the courts... It must be understood that the judiciary and the forces of law and order are organised in hierarchical layers, and it is here that Masonic *interference* comes into play when it comes to shedding light on this or that case, particularly in cases involving paedocriminal networks. At certain levels of the hierarchy, institutional protections are automatic and maximum as long as these pawns are subject to the diktat of their own vices (held by compromising files)...

Journalists, for their part, have understood that this area of investigation is highly risky and has been blackballed by the major newsrooms for the past fifteen years. The explosive France 3 documentary *"Viols d'enfants: la fin du silence"* (*"Child rape: the end of silence"*) recounted the testimonies of Pierre and Marie, two children who recounted how they had allegedly taken part in paedo-satanic ceremonies involving ritual child sacrifices in a subterranean structure in the Paris region. It was on this occasion that the former deputy public prosecutor in Bobigny, Martine Bouillon, declared on Élise Lucet's show that she knew of mass graves of children discovered in the Paris region... without being able to say more because of the ongoing investigation.

Martine Bouillon was disciplined by her superiors the following day. She was dismissed by the senior magistrate Michel Joubrel... who was later himself indicted for possession of child pornography, including photos of babies under the age of 2, according to investigators...

Many journalists are aware of the existence of these ultra-violent networks, and know full well that they have everything to lose (their social life, their professional life, even their own life) if they attack something like this. Others are certainly in denial, making their lives easier... Especially as today, in the age of atheism and widespread relativism, the question of paedo-satanism is, for many, a *conspiracy theory of the witch-hunt* type.

From that point on, they dismiss this type of case out of hand, even though there is plenty to investigate.

Politically and in the media, child pornography networks do not exist... There are only "isolated predators" or "image consumers" on the Internet... As for the networks producing child pornography, they are never bothered!

The first thing to do for the brave newcomer to the subject is to begin by studying the textbook case of the Dutroux affair in Belgium. There you'll find institutional corruption (police and judiciary), the question of the network, *satanic* practices in the upper echelons of society (with the X witnesses), mental control based on trauma (with Régina Louf), and also the role of the mainstream media, which all played the same score in chorus: the - official - version of the isolated predator, shamefully dismissing the version, however obvious, of a vast network involving *big fish*...

It is clear that the harshness and horror of such a repulsive subject provokes the first and natural reflex of an individual, which is rejection and denial... This does not facilitate progress in terms of research, justice and help for victims.

Faced with such horrors that call into question an entire societal paradigm, many people prefer to turn a blind eye, even when the evidence is there...

Dr Petra Murkel described this phenomenon well on Arte's Xenius programme:

"We want to hear stories that are clear and plausible, but the truth is often an obstacle. It may seem too complicated, or it may not correspond to our moral values or simply our expectations. We lie to ourselves... The truth can be a source of despair, whereas a lie can carry us for a very long time. Researchers have also shown that intelligent self-manipulation is essential to the joy of living: it gives us meaning and structure. From an evolutionary point of view, this is obviously an advantage, because a lifelong lie gives us strength for a long time.

Appendix 1

Jung & Mozart: two childhoods initiated into traumatic rituals?

Illumination does not consist in perceiving luminous forms or visions, but in making the darkness visible... C.G. Yung

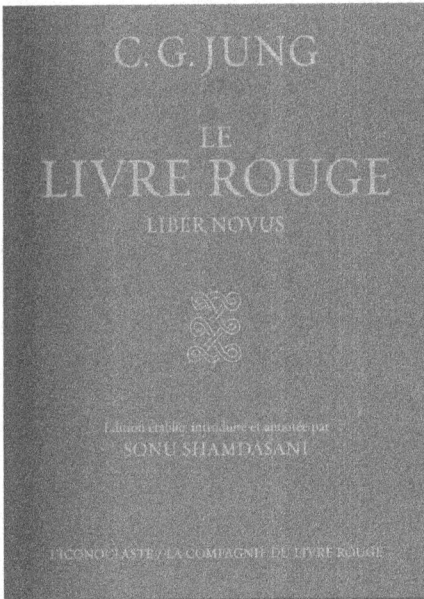

In her book *Answer to Jung: Making sense of the Red Book* Lynn Brunet argues that Carl Gustav Jung's famous mystical work, soberly titled *'The Red Book'*, contains numerous references to the Masonic symbolism of the high degrees, mainly of the Scottish Rite. Written between 1914 and 1930, but first published in 2009, it is considered one of the major works of psychology. In it, Jung recorded his dreams and fantasies during a period of confrontation with the unconscious when he literally thought he was going mad, in a *schizophrenic* state he would say... With its calligraphic texts, images, paintings, mandalas and an astonishing wealth of imaginary characters and mythology, the Red Book tells the story of a man who **must rediscover his myth and who sets off in search of his lost soul.**

The philosopher Françoise Bonardel talks about the Red Book in these terms: *"What Jung describes here is a journey of initiation... One day he begins to have visions, revelations of sorts, and figures appear who speak to him.* ***He describes this journey into the depths of his unconscious with extremely violent sequences, which resemble an initiatory killing scenario!*** *Particularly when he descends into the depths and almost drowns in a kind of lake of blood (...)* ***It's all a descent into hell, he goes through a lot (...) This is the very example of a journey of initiation and a savage initiation, carried out by someone who has nevertheless managed to stay on course and not sink into madness".*** (Le Livre Rouge, un voyage initiatique - BaglisTV)

Lynn Brunet notes in the preface to her book: "Through my own childhood initiation memories and my research into Masonic ritual abuse, I quickly drew parallels between Jung's writings and the initiation ordeals. It was then very revealing when I read *Memories, Dreams, Reflections* and discovered that **his paternal grandfather was a Freemason, Worshipful Master of the Basel Lodge (...) This raises the possibility that Jung could be yet another victim of Masonic ritual abuse. My question in this study is this: Could The Red Book be a detailed account of a series of memoirs, albeit extremely confused and confusing ones, about initiations undergone as a child and found in contemporary accounts of ritual abuse?**

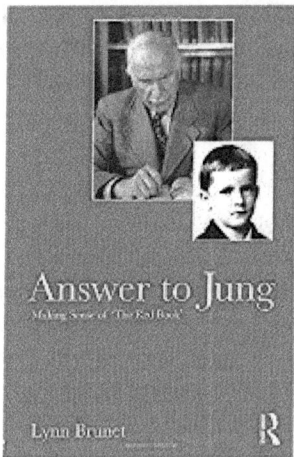

In a lecture entitled *"Carl Gustav Jung and Freemasonry"*, the poet, writer and editor Jean-Luc Maxence tells us that Jung's father, a modest pastor, was also a Freemason: *"Can it really be said that Jung was greatly influenced by Freemasonry from an early age, and that he even established the major concepts of his clinic, depth psychology, all inhabited, whether consciously or not, by the great symbols of Masonry?* **One thing is certain: from an early age, as a child and then as an adolescent, Jung was physically surrounded by speculative Freemasons.** *There was the influence of his grandfather, Karl Gustav Jung Senior (...) as for his father, as everyone knows a mediocre pastor, a theologian who was a bit of a Jack-of-all-trades,* **he was also** *a Freemason..."*.

Here we find a form of transgenerational Masonry, where successive generations are systematically inducted into the Lodge from father to son... the question of the passage of children through traumatic initiation rituals remains (at the level of the upper hierarchy). Several sources report that his ancestor Johann Sigismund, known as Sigismund von Jung, a lawyer, was also a Freemason and a member of the "*Illuminati* of Bavaria".

Here is the back cover of Lynn Brunet's book: The Red Book is Jung's account of a period of deep introspection into his unconscious in a process he called *'active imagination'*, undertaken in mid-life. *Answer to Jung: Making Sense of 'The Red Book'* offers a close reading of this beautiful and disturbing text and its fascinating images, and demonstrates that the fantasies of the Red Book are not entirely original, **but that their plots, characters and symbols are remarkably similar to certain rituals of the high degrees of Freemasonry. The book argues that these fantasies may be memories of a series of** terrifying initiatory ordeals, possibly undergone in childhood, using altered or spurious versions of Masonic rites. The book then compares these initiation scenarios with accounts of traumatic rituals reported since the 1980s.

Dr James Randall Noblitt notes in his book *Cult and Ritual Abuse* about Jung and his Red Book: "*During the period when Carl Jung was engaged in his own inner exploration, in a 'confrontation with his subconscious', he archived his thoughts and mental imagery in a series of Black Books, which were later assembled to form his Red Book. This content was never published during his lifetime, and would only be shared confidentially with a select group of people.* This remarkable volume was kept hidden by Jung's family after his death, until it was finally published in 2009. On page 290 of the Red Book is a paragraph entitled **The Sacrificial Murder**, referring to a ritual in which a child is killed. In this scene, Jung describes himself eating a piece of the child's liver after being ordered to do so. Jung himself acknowledges that in this horrific act he too was sacrificed.*"

His own autobiography **portrays** Jung, his mother and his cousin, Helena Preiswerk, **as having experiences of dissociation of identity**. Lynn Brunet also reports that one of Jung's biographers, Claire Dunne, refers to the revelation he made to Sigmund Freud about being raped as a child. Dunne used this tragic episode as the title of her book Jung: *Wounded* Healer *of the Soul*.

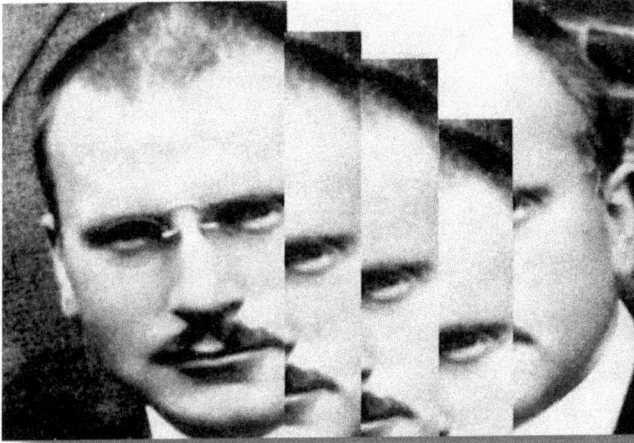

The wound from which Jung seems to have been healed could be much deeper than that... The frequent expressions of *pain, suffering, confusion* and *torment* in the Red Book explicitly suggest that it deals with the question of trauma and that the interpretation of its symbolic contents would need to incorporate the psychology and physiology of trauma. Jung was very familiar with the physiological concepts of dissociation, amnesia and trauma...

Wolfgang Amadeus Mozart is also one of the *great men* of history who was immersed in Masonic circles from childhood. The religious scholar and musicologist Carl de Nys, who devoted

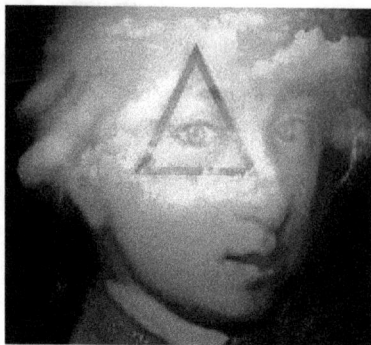

a large part of his life to studying Mozart's work, reports that , having grown up in Slazburg, was deeply imbued with Masonic ideas. **At the time, there was a flourishing of Masonic lodges in the region, such as the Bavarian Illuminati, better known as the "*illuminati*".** The environment in which Mozart grew up was totally imbued with this occult spirituality. Carl de Nys tells us that these Bavarian illuminati often held their meetings in the park de Aigen in Salzburg. They turned it into a sort of forest of the gods, with altars, funerary monuments and so on. **At the time, the park belonged to one of their members, a close friend of the Mozarts... The initiation ceremony took place in the "*Witches' Hole*": a cave whose entrance was flanked by two columns supporting a symbol of the Mysteries of Isis, i.e. a winged Sphinx... According to tradition, this cave had been used by the followers of Mithras and Astarte since Roman times.** Initiation ceremonies took place at night and the cave was lit by torches, which is exactly the setting for the "ordeal" scene in the second act of *The Magic Flute*. **Carl de Nys claims, with supporting sources, that the young Mozart took part in "*night meetings*" in this cave in the park at Aigen**, and that it was this that inspired his initiation scene... (*Mozart chez les francs-maçons* - les archives de la RTS, 02/01/90)

Grotte des *illuminati* (Hexenloch) près du château d'Aigen, Salzbourg

According to Carl de Nys, the Mozart family was linked to the Bavarian Lodge of the Illuminati, which seemed to practise the initiation rites of the ancient Mystery religions, particularly the Mysteries of Isis.

Caves and caverns were ideal places for dark initiations. Éliphas Lévi (a French ecclesiastic and occultist born Alphonse-Louis Constant) describes certain ancient initiation rituals as follows: "*The great trials of **Memphis and Eleusis** were intended to train kings and priests by entrusting science to courageous and strong men. To be admitted to these ordeals, you had to devote yourself body and soul to the priesthood and give up your life. **You had to descend into dark underground tunnels** where you had to cross burning pyres, streams of deep, fast-flowing water, movable bridges thrown over abysses, and all without letting a lamp you were holding in your hand go out or escape. Those who faltered or were afraid were never to see the light again; those who intrepidly overcame all the obstacles were **received** among the mystics, **that is to say they were initiated into the minor mysteries. But his fidelity and silence remained to be tested, and it was only after several years that he became an epopt, a title that corresponds to that of adept** (...) It is not in the books of the philosophers, but in the religious symbolism of the ancients that* *we must seek the traces of science and rediscover its mysteries (...)* **All the true initiates have recognised the immense usefulness of work and pain. Pain," said a German poet, "is the dog of the unknown shepherd who leads the flock of men. Learning to suffer, learning to die, is the gymnastics of Eternity, the immortal novitiate".** ("*The History of Magic*" - Éliphas Lévi, 1999, p.122)

The ancient Greeks were well aware of **the effects of profound physiological stress in altering an individual's perceptions of the world. Ancient Greek priests used traumatic rituals to 'cure' certain patients. To do this, they had them descend into the cave of** *Trophonios*... The person was prepared for this rite by fasting, lustration (a water purification ceremony) and sleep deprivation. They were then lowered into the underground chamber and left alone in complete darkness. The intoxicating gases exhaled in this cavern, or possibly the lack of oxygen, soon had an effect on the person, provoking terrible dreams and visions. Just in time, she would be rescued from the cave and brought out into the light and fresh air.

This kind of ordeal caused a real trauma that was supposed to cure the patient. Psychiatrist William Sargant has no hesitation in using the term *"brainwashing"* to describe the rituals of the oracle *of Trophonios*, during which the subject was subjected to sensory deprivation, visual and auditory confusion techniques and psychotropic drugs. Just as we go to a psychiatrist today when we need advice or treatment, the ancient Greeks consulted oracles for the same purpose . Before going to see the oracle, the person first had to experience sleep deprivation, repetitive chanting, taking drugs and finally venturing alone into deep, dark caverns. **This long and exhausting struggle, which could last several days, put her in a state of extreme physiological stress**. Then, when the oracle revealed certain things to them, they were able to understand their meaning **thanks to this altered state of consciousness, which gave them a different view of the world** (*"Source for the Study of Greek Religion"* - David Rice, John Stambaugh, 1979, p.144).

Carl de Nys asserts that the Bavarian Illuminati of Salzburg performed their initiation ceremonies in a grotto whose entrance was flanked by two columns supporting a winged Sphinx, the symbol of the Mysteries of Isis... In his work entitled

"Metamorphoses", the writer Apuleius seems to describe **his own initiation into the Mysteries of Isis and Osiris**, to which he is said to have been initiated during his stay in Greece: "*The high priest then dismissed the profane, dressed me in an unbleached linen robe and, taking me by the hand, **led me into the deepest part of the sanctuary**. No doubt, my dear reader, your curiosity will be aroused by what is said and what is done next. I would say it if I were allowed to say it; you would learn it if you were allowed to learn it. But it would be a crime to the same degree for the ears of the confidant and for the mouth of the revelator. If, however, it is a religious feeling that motivates you, I would scruple to torment you. Listen and believe, for what I say is true. **I have touched the gates of death; my foot rested on Proserpine's threshold. On my return I crossed the elements. In the depths of the night I saw the sun shine. Gods of hell, gods of the Empyrean, all have been seen by me face to face**, and adored at close quarters. This is what I have to tell you, and you will be no more enlightened.*"

So here we find three essential components of Masonic-type secret societies: **death and resurrection, trial by the elements**

and, finally, enlightenment. It is possible that this is a traumatic ritual involving the candidate for initiation in an experience bordering on death *(I touched the gates of death)* with a profound state of dissociation *illuminating* his consciousness *(I saw the sun shine)*.

What initiation rites might little Mozart have undergone when he was taken to the *"Witches' Hole"* by these illuminated Bavarians or *Illuminati*?

Masonic Temple of Fraternity and Union in Rennes (35)

Appendix 2

Trauma and Dissociation in Masonic Mythology

Extracts from the book *"Terror, Trauma and The Eye In The Triangle"* Lynn Brunet - 2007, p. 64 to 83

The Masonic Presence
in Contemporary Art

Initiatory Themes and Trauma

lynn Brunet.

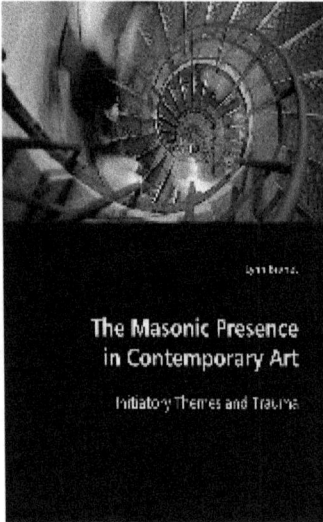

Solomon's Temple has often been interpreted as a metaphor for the human body. Freemason author Albert Mackey confirms this when he writes: "Third degree ceremonies in which a dilapidated building metaphorically represents the deterioration and infirmities associated with old age in the human body." The two columns, Jakin and Boaz, represent the entrance to the Temple. In Kabbalistic literature, these two pillars correspond to the right and left sides of the body with their mirror effect (...) This is where we find the link with the left and right functions of the human brain, which each control the opposite side of the body - this is controlaterality. These two pillars can also represent qualities such as severity and clemency, the concept of black and white, Adam and Eve, male and female, etc...

Solomon's Temple was intended to provide a permanent home for the Ark of the Covenant, which since the time of Moses had been housed in a tent (...) In a plan of Solomon's Temple, depicted in a Masonic document entitled "*The Two Pillars*", the Ark of the Covenant is located in the Holy of Holies with the incense altar next to it.

(editor's note: Lynn Brunet draws a parallel between the Ark of the Covenant and the thalamus, a structure at the heart of the brain)

The word thalamus is derived from the Greek word for "inner chamber", commonly used as a bridal chamber. The thalamus is located in the centre of the brain, is completely covered by the cortical hemisphere and is the main gateway that relays sensory information to the cerebral cortex; the main input streams to the cortex must pass through the thalamus. As Francis Cricks notes, *"The idea that the thalamus is a key to consciousness is not new. Its role is to maintain harmony between the somatosensory system and an individual's mental and emotional activity"*. He also notes that a large part of the thalamus is called the 'pulvinar', a word that originally meant a 'cushion' or 'pillow' (...) another variation means 'sacred couch' or 'seat of honour'.

Could this choice of terminology refer to the throne of grace of the Ark of the Covenant housed in the Holy of Holies? If so, the positioning of the incense altar right next to the Holy of Holies could be a symbolic reference to the fact that the sense of smell is the only sense that does not involve a crossing of the nerve pathways between the brain and the body: the right side of the nose is connected to the right side of the brain. The close relationship between the sense of smell and memory is well known (...) When Solomon recreated a 'house' for the Ark, he placed the cherubim in such a way that their wings touched the side of each wall. In physiological terms, the wings of the cherubim can symbolically represent the two sides of the cerebral cortex that touch the inside of the skull walls and meet face to face in the inner chamber where consciousness resides. Seen in this way, the 'Throne of Grace' could then symbolically represent the brain's ability to organise chaos, i.e. the continuous mass of incoming sensory information processed instantaneously by the thalamus (...).) The Middle Chamber (which marks the end of the initiation of the first three Masonic degrees: Apprentice, Companion and Master) and its spiral staircase are two important Masonic symbols (...) Mackey writes that the Companions, the workers in the Temple, climb the spiral staircase to reach the Middle Chamber. He interprets this Middle Chamber as the place where Truth is received and the spiral staircase as a symbol of spiritual progression.

Research on the thalamus has shown that it contains a number of activity centres, known as 'nuclei'. The main one is called the 'ventral caudal (or posterior) nucleus'. Neurologist Chihiro Ohye writes that "within the ventral caudal nucleus is an area called the ventral intermediate nucleus, which contains scattered clusters of cells. Electrical stimulation of this part of the nucleus induces a sensation of spinning or elevation, a kind of ascent." (...) Psychologist Susan Blackmore states that certain hallucinogenic experiences can have an impact on brain cells by producing a vision composed of spiral stripes that can appear like a tunnel on the visual cortex. In physiological terms, the spiral staircase symbol may therefore be a way of illustrating this physical feeling of spinning and ascending with this hallucinatory vision. As for this place where 'Truth' is received, it is possible that this Middle Chamber could be a familiar place for those who study meditation, an area of the brain that is neither to the right nor to the left, a state of totally centred calm where the individual can feel a sense of connection with the divine (...).)
Located somewhere in the thalamus, the inner room or 'nuptial chamber' may be another way of representing the mystical concept of alchemical marriage (or chymical nuptials), represented as the concept of the hermaphrodite, or in Jungian terms, a condition in which the masculine and feminine aspects of the psyche are in total harmony (...)

In terms of traumatology, the Hiram legend can be seen as a metaphorical text that represents what happens physiologically when terror is used to produce the experience of *inner light*. This *inner light* is that sense of cosmic consciousness or immortality that is attained through the slow spiritual ascent represented in the Second Degree. Freemasonry belongs to the Gnostic tradition. The figure of Lucifer, the "Bringer of Light", the light of mystical experience, is at the heart of this tradition. The relationship between Lucifer and the psychology

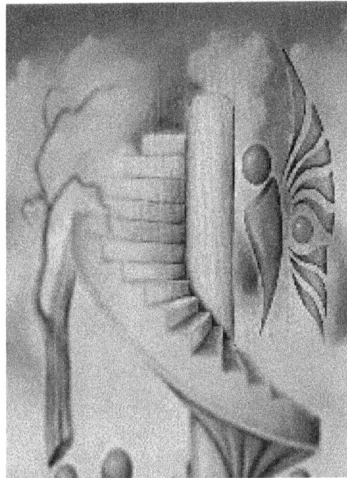

of trauma is highlighted in a play entitled "The Tragedy of Man", written by Hungarian playwright Imre Madach and analysed by anthropologist Geza Roheim. Lucifer, the play's central character, is called "the Spirit of Denial". In the play, Lucifer invites Adam to fly into space (i.e. to dissociate himself from reality) in order to escape the scum of earthly life: "*Pain will cease when we give in and the last link that binds us to Mother Earth disappears*".

This human ability to escape terror and intense emotional or physical pain through denial and dissociation may have been exploited by Freemasonry to achieve mystical experiences. By interfering with the cerebral process through physical or psychic trauma (shock, terror, hypnosis), the mind can undergo a disruption of the notion of time and experience a feeling of timelessness (...)

The myth of Isis and Osiris, used in the Scottish Rite, can also be a metaphorical illustration of the traumatic process. Mackey writes that "*Osiris was killed by a typhoon and his body cut into pieces, his mutilated remains thrown into the Nile and scattered to the four winds. His wife Isis, mourning the death and mutilation of her husband, searched for the body parts for several days, and after finding them, she reunited the pieces to give him a decent burial. Osiris, thus restored, became one of the main Egyptian deities, and his cult joined with that of Isis to form a fertile deity for the*

fertilisation of nature" (...) If we interpret the characters Isis and Osiris in terms of brain structures, Isis represents the right brain, the intuitive attributes, and Osiris represents the left brain, the logical and linguistic attributes.

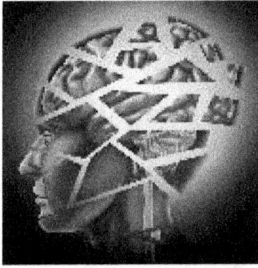

Damage caused by trauma can lead to memory recording problems in the left hemisphere and can therefore affect the individual's ability to talk about the events they have experienced, as the transfer of information from the right brain is "mutilated" or fragmented. It is then difficult for the individual to reconstitute the fragments of memory, which are like pieces of a jigsaw puzzle. These Egyptian gods could be interpreted as embodying this phenomenon of memory disorders in a fragmented mind following a traumatic experience.

References to mutilation or self-mutilation among the mythological gods abound in the magical and religious literature of ancient Egypt. The self-inflicted mutilations of the gods are generally due to emotional stress of various kinds. Budge notes that in other scenarios relating to the theme of death and resurrection in the Osirian myth of Horus, son of Isis and Osiris, Horus has the role of restoring life in an embrace, a gesture reminiscent of the 'Five Points of Masonic Companionship'. *"Horus came to Osiris, who was in the state of a dead man, and embraced him. By this embrace he transferred to him his own KA (double), or part of the power that dwelt in it. The embrace is in fact an act by which the vital energy is transferred from the embracer to the embraced"*. Budge observes that the embrace can also be metaphorically considered as a restoration of information in the linguistic centre of the left brain for the purpose of psychic healing after a major trauma. Alan Watt, studying the theme of fractionation in the myth of Osiris and other ancient myths, argues that the sacrificial dismemberment of a divine being is a voluntary process, that of self-sacrifice. He writes: *"It logically follows that where there is a dismemberment (deconstruction) at the beginning, there is a reconstruction at the end* (editor's note: Ordo ab Chao or Dissolve then Coagulate) *It is the cosmic game that consists in the discovery of what is hidden and the remembrance of what has been dispersed."*

Watt's conclusion relates to a notion about memory in spiritual processes and the role of concentration in reducing scattered thoughts. I would argue that this myth is even more appropriate when applied to the nature of traumatic memory, its repression and recollection (...) The Freemason Leadbeater suggests that initiation in its purest form involves a kind of connection with the divine and this is what the different Masonic degrees represent. The 'tearing into fragments' suggests that initiation requires an understanding of the use of shocks to produce a certain state of consciousness, which if produced correctly, can create the sensation of being 'one with the universe'. Such a state of consciousness is now considered by the medical field to be an example of a state of dissociation. Casavis, in an analysis of the Greek origins of Freemasonry, notes the role of fragmentation in the Osirian Mysteries. He notes that the sacred plant of this

Mystery cult was Erica, from the Greek word 'eriko' meaning 'to *break into pieces*'.

Freemason Albert Mackey reports that the Egyptian symbol most relevant to Freemasonry is that of the "all-seeing eye", mystically interpreted as the eye of God, , but also as a *symbol of divine vigilance and care for the universe.* The adoption of the equilateral triangle is a symbol of divinity that can be found throughout different cultures. Mackey writes: "*Among the Egyptians, the hare was the hieroglyph for open eyes, which is so because this fragile animal is supposed never to close its organs of vision; it is always on the lookout for its enemies. The hare was then adopted by priests as a symbol of the mental illumination or mystical light that is revealed to neophytes as they contemplate divine truth during their initiation. And so, according to Champollian, the hare was also the symbol of Osiris, a principal god, thus showing the close link between the*

initiation process in their sacred rites and the contemplation of the divine nature."

One of the consequences of severe trauma is a state known as "hypervigilance". This is a state of constant attention and exhausting fear, where the victim, like the rabbit or the hare, is constantly on the lookout for danger. When Osiris was resurrected, he possessed the "all-seeing eye". If the reconstruction of Osiris represents the recovery of traumatic memories, then this ability to "see everything" can be translated as the ability to face death or evil. These notions of facing death, the idea of the journey and rebirth in Masonic texts therefore take on a certain significance with contemporary theories on memory and trauma. From a physiological point of view, it is interesting to note that the neurons that seem to be most associated with consciousness are described as pyramidal cells.

We can draw a parallel with the symbolism of Isaac Newton's discovery of the decomposition of white light into the different colours of the rainbow through a triangular glass prism. The eye in the Masonic triangle embodies Newton's physics in the sense that it can be a visual representation of splitting, referring to dissociation, the illumination of consciousness (...)

Here, the Enlightenment philosophy on the link between Terror and the Sublime described by Edmund Burke becomes relevant. All things that convey terror, he says, "*are a source of the Sublime, they produce the strongest emotion the mind is capable of feeling.*" Perhaps this echoes neurological research. The place where all these functions seem to coordinate is called the limbic system, comprising the thalamus, amygdala, hippocampus and other structures. As Pierre-Marie Lledo puts it: "*Like the limbo of Christian mythology, the limbic system is the intermediary between the neo-mammalian brain of paradise and the reptilian brain of hell.*" (...)

On the 21st degree Masonic apron, the Noachite or Prussian Grade is a winged human holding the index finger of his right hand to his lips and a key in his left hand. This representation is known as the Egyptian figure of Silence (...) In the Masonic system, the Tower of Babel is an image linked to memories and forgetting, linked to confusion and the loss of language. According to the Freemasons: "*Passing in front of the Tower makes you forget everything you know*" (...) The winged figure of Silence on the

21st degree Masonic apron can also represent this process of dissociation. The inability to talk about the traumatic experience is represented by the right index finger held in front of the mouth, the right hand being controlled by the left brain, the side of the brain that affects language. The left hand (symbolising access to the right side of the brain where the dissociated traumatic memories are stored) holds the 'key' to these memories.

The stories of the Flood and the Tower of Babel can be interpreted as another metaphor for how the brain functions during trauma. In much of the literature on trauma, the experience is described as "leaving the body", a phenomenon linked to the process of dissociation. A sense of peace is felt as the person psychically disconnects from the terror, finding a natural way to escape. The flight of the 'soul' from the body in traumatic situations is represented by the release of the dove from Noah's Ark and symbolises, in physiological terms, the opioid effect released in the brain when terror 'floods' the physical body (...).(...) After the Flood (of terror), the rainbow (dissociated identity) then becomes a symbol of hope because the flood of terror is forgotten and the individual can survive (...) Individuals' lives become psychologically 'divided' after they have experienced something that could have killed them. In cabbalistic texts, the rainbow is also linked to the Way of the Chameleon, the animal that changes colour according to its environment. This is linked to the phenomenon of multiple personality, where the individual is able to adapt to different situations with distinct personalities (alter or fragments of personality). All this symbolism gives rise to the possibility that the story of Noah's Ark and the Ark of the Covenant may also correspond to metaphors for processes linked to the human brain...

Appendix 3

Definition of trauma-induced dissociation

Extract from the dissertation *"L'Abus Rituel : Le point de vue d'intervenantes en agression sexuelle"*, presented by Christine Jacques in 2008 at the Université du Québec en Outaouais in the Department of Social Work.

Ritual abuse is still a subject about which very little is known in the various intervention environments. The lack of consensus on how to conceptualise ritual abuse and the controversy surrounding it hinder its recognition. This qualitative research has three objectives: to document and analyse information about ritual abuse, to advance knowledge and understanding of this type of abuse from the point of view of sexual assault workers who have supported women who have experienced it since early childhood, and to contribute to the advancement of knowledge on the subject in the French-speaking intervention community. Semi-structured interviews were conducted with eight sexual assault counsellors who work in different sexual assault services and who admitted to having worked with at least two survivors of ritual (...)

It is also recommended that more research be carried out on ritual abuse, particularly with regard to programming, a method of thought control, and dissociation in ritual abuse survivors. Above all, needs to develop more practical knowledge of intervention in this field. More research is also needed into the links between ritual abuse and sexual sadism, and between ritual abuse and child sexual exploitation networks.

UQO
UNIVERSITÉ
DU QUÉBEC
EN OUTAOUAIS

Dissociation

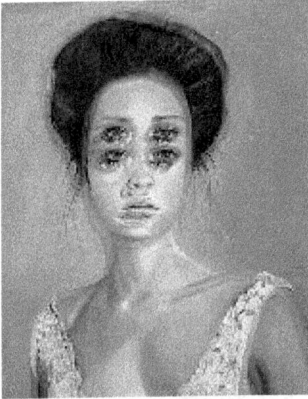

All the participants talked about dissociation when discussing the after-effects. It should be remembered that some of them acknowledged that individuals who commit ritual abuse provoke dissociation in the people they abuse in order to gain greater control over them. Nonetheless, the majority of participants (6/8) saw dissociation above all as a normal and essential defence mechanism that enables victims to survive the intensity of the abuse and the ensuing trauma.

Kluft, Herman, Putnam and others have done much to define dissociation and the criteria for its most extreme form: dissociative identity disorder, formerly known as multiple personality disorder. They identified this disorder in particular with the presence of dissociative amnesic barriers, causing fragmentation of the 'self' and the presence of several distinct personalities - or alter identities - that have been created to overcome an intolerable trauma, usually severe childhood abuse. (Beardsley, 2002, p. 111)

It should also be remembered that, unlike the psychiatric approach, the participants do not consider dissociation to be a mental disorder or disorder. They therefore use the term dissociation or multiple personalities to deal with the subject rather than dissociative disorders as presented in the American Psychiatric Association's Mini DSM-IV (1994) diagnostic criteria or the Mini Manual of Diagnostic Criteria. They do, however, testify to the consequences of this defence mechanism in the current lives of women who have developed it. In addition, half of them deal with the way dissociation is used in ritual abuse.

Half of the participants gave a brief explanation of dissociation. One of them said that dissociation is one of the most important impacts of ritual abuse and that children who are victims learn to dissociate. "*The child dissociates at a very early age because something intolerable is happening. His mind separates and the child dissociates in order to manage and cope with something that would otherwise be impossible to manage.*

Dissociation can manifest itself to different degrees. Some participants (3/8) spoke of dissociation consisting of an inability to recall personal memories, past or recent, while others (5/8) spoke more specifically of what they considered to be a more extreme degree of dissociation, namely what they called "multiple personalities". It should be noted that dissociation in the form of multiple personalities arises only from trauma suffered in early childhood.

Dissociation, which manifests itself as an inability to recall memories, means that some ritual abuse survivors have very few memories of their childhood. One of the participants spoke of amnesia, saying that survivors may have blocked out certain memories relating to the traumas they suffered; their memories generally arise during flashbacks. Another participant spoke of the inability of some survivors to recall more recent memories. Dissociation means that survivors can sometimes lose touch with the present and feel as though they are reliving traumatic moments from their past. Women who dissociate in this way may be in this state for a few hours or even a few days. These women are no longer fully aware or in control of what they are doing during this period and may find themselves in situations they would not necessarily take on if they were not in a dissociative state.

More than half of the participants (5/8) said that the ritual abuse survivors they work with often have multiple personalities. Here's how one of them explained it:

"Extreme dissociation, or more specifically the formation of what is known as multiple personalities, or what others call dissociative identity disorder, means that the survivor has divided her mind into several parts and separated them from each other so that she can, for example, experience torture during the night and the next day be completely unaware of what she has been through... The next day, she'll be able to go to school and perform in a relatively normal way because two or more parts will have been involved. One of them takes over outside the conscious of the first party. Survivors may therefore have two or more different identities that are separate in the unconscious from each other."

For example, survivors of ritual abuse may sometimes appear to be living a normal life, going to school or having a job, but in fact they can only cope with their lives as a function of the dissociative abilities they developed during the trauma they suffered. It's as if these people are living a double life. This way of managing their daily lives corresponds to one of the elements of the concept of dissociation according to van der Hart, Nijenhuis and Steele (2006):

"Chronically traumatised individuals are caught in a terrible dilemma. They do not have the capacity for adequate integration and the mental skills to consciously and fully realise their terrifying experiences. They have to get on with their daily lives, which sometimes even include the people who abused them. The quickest option for them is to mentally put aside their painful past and present and as far as possible maintain a facade of normality".

Like these authors, the participant who said that ritual abuse survivors live as if they had a double life stressed that there is stress created by behaving as if everything were normal.

The most extreme form of dissociation, multiple personalities, means that a person's identity is divided or fragmented into two or more 'parts'. They are one and the same person, but their identity is constructed in a divided way. The term "multiplicity" is commonly used to deal with this subject, as is the word "parts" to refer to these different divisions of the personality. The different parts of the identity are distinct in the sense that they present different aspects, characteristics or states of personality. Each part has its own modalities, i.e. knowledge, ways of being, acting, thinking, feeling, perceiving oneself, conceiving the environment and situating oneself in time. In addition, the parts are separated in the unconscious and are not necessarily aware of each other. As a result, some parts are unaware of the abuse they have suffered, while others retain memories of the experience.

More than half of the participants (5/8) described certain ways in which dissociation or multiplicity presents itself in ritual abuse survivors. The woman, or 'host' part, may simply mention what inner voices tell her, while others will testify about their 'inner parts'. They may also say that they are beginning to lose track of time, or that they have always lost track of time. The term hostess is used to refer to extreme dissociation and to identify the woman or the part that is present at the intervention meetings. One of the participants explained that the term "inner parts" used to describe extreme dissociation refers to people with multiple personalities who have developed what is known as a "dissociative system", i.e. a system of inner parts. The use of the word "system", often used to refer to multiplicity, is equivalent to the whole person; all the inner parts of the person are therefore taken into consideration.

They also describe the differences they have observed between each of the parts of ritual abuse survivors who have developed multiple personalities. "You can see in women with multiple personalities how different each part is; some parts are right-handed, others left-handed. Some women can even demonstrate physical changes when certain parts present themselves."

Half of the participants said that the child parties came to them. They said that it was mostly the children who told them about the abuse they had suffered. One of them said that sometimes it was as if another person was speaking: a child's voice, a boy or a girl. Another said that the parties could also use different first names when introducing themselves.

It is important to point out that all the practitioners interviewed spoke of the dissociation that ritual abuse survivors still experience. Dissociation is an impact that is present at the time of the abuse and continues into adulthood. Half of them said they had never met a ritual abuse survivor for whom dissociation was not an issue. Some (3/8) said that some of the survivors they worked with had already been diagnosed with one of the disorders associated with dissociation before meeting them.

However, one of the participants cautioned that although many ritual abuse survivors have developed multiple personalities, it is important not to generalise. For example, she said that she had accompanied two sisters who had suffered ritual abuse and that only one of them had developed multiple personalities.

Despite the fact that all the participants considered dissociation to be a normal defence mechanism, more than half of them (5/8) acknowledged that it can become an obstacle for survivors. It is sometimes difficult for ritual abuse survivors who dissociate or who have multiple personalities to stay in touch with the present. This loss of awareness of the present moment is one of the factors in the dissociation that currently affects ritual abuse survivors. Here's how one of the participants explains some of the difficulties experienced by ritual abuse survivors with multiple personalities: "Certain parts of themselves can live in the past. This can be very difficult to work through. Some women have no memory of their parts; that's also difficult to work on. How can a woman connect when she loses track of time, when she doesn't know one of her parts and when that part doesn't show up when she follows up with you?"

Two other participants explained that dissociation makes the healing process more complex for some ritual abuse survivors, as they dissociate or continually experience flashbacks. This limits their ability to become fully aware of their reality. These counsellors spoke above all of the powerlessness caused by dissociation, particularly in women with multiple personalities. Another said that dissociation makes ritual abuse survivors more vulnerable and more at risk of reliving other situations of abuse because they are not in full control of themselves. One woman explains what she considers to be one of the particularities of dissociation resulting from ritual abuse. In her view, ritual abuse "is always there, it's never in the past, it's always there. Even if the abusers are not there, the memories are so fresh and dissociation brings them back as if they were still there". So dissociation, which was necessary for the survival of victims of ritual abuse, can now be an obstacle in their current lives.

It should be remembered that some participants (3/8) said that abusers know and use victims' dissociative abilities. Dissociation makes victims more suggestible and this vulnerability facilitates the programming process. They believe that offenders check victims' dissociative abilities and that this enables them to determine the best ways to provoke this mechanism in order to control them on an ongoing basis.

Appendix 4

Trauma-based mental control

Extract from the dissertation "*L'Abus Rituel : Le point de vue d'intervenantes en agression sexuelle*", presented by Christine Jacques in 2008 at the Université du Québec en Outaouais in the Department of Social Work.

The methods used for programming

As presented in the theoretical framework, thought control techniques are the cornerstone of ritual abuse. This research shows us that the practitioners interviewed mainly use the term programming to talk about the subject.

According to the results obtained, the methods used for programming are the first clues that ritual abuse is involved. This is consistent with the importance attached to the way in which the abuse is carried out. We believe that these are the main characteristics of ritual abuse that distinguish it from other forms of abuse. In this sense, we recognise that the methods used for programming are the elements that shock, surprise and give a bizarre appearance to the survivors' accounts.

It should be remembered that the results relating to programming deal with two distinct elements: the aim of the programming and the methods used to achieve it.

According to the results obtained, the programming aims to transform the victims' sense of identity and freedom, and to create a feeling of continuous terror, in order to obtain absolute and continuous control over their person. These findings support those concerning the purpose of ritual abuse. In the light of the results obtained, we can say that the methods used to program the victims of ritual abuse are abuse techniques carefully chosen by the abusers. These results are consistent with those concerning the organised nature of ritual abuse and the after-effects that result.

The participants say that terror is at the very root of the programming. Among other things, the abusers use various threats to create a feeling of constant danger in the victims. The results show that child victims of ritual abuse are threatened with death if they talk about the abuse they have suffered. They are also threatened either with being abused again or with harm being done to people close to them. In other words, victims of ritual abuse are programmed to believe that they are in constant danger. It is by comparing all the results obtained that it becomes possible to understand that this feeling of persistent threat stems above all from the terror created by the abuse suffered during childhood. In addition to programming, the traumas suffered and dissociation mean that the intensity of the feeling of terror, conditioned during childhood, persists into adulthood. As many of the results show, this feeling of ongoing danger is programmed to silence the victims and hide the reality of the criminal activities committed in ritual abuse. In this sense, it is through the silence they impose that abusers maintain absolute and continuous power over their victims.

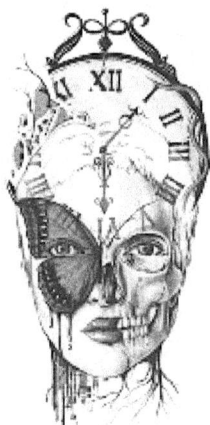

The results relating to programming correspond to the information presented by Borelli (2006) following her documentary research on the subject. Among others, she cites Oglevie (2003), who outlines the three principles of thought control: secrecy, power and control. According to this author: *People who use mind control are obsessed with power... These people perpetuate and instil mind control through fear and panic in their subjects* (quoted by Borelli, 2006, p.54). What's more: *When abusers use mind control, the victims' silence is virtually guaranteed.* (Ibid, p. 55). This information demonstrates the link between programming and the secret and clandestine nature of ritual abuse.

The results obtained in the course of this research also show that programming is the backdrop to each form of abuse. We agree with the participants who say that what characterises ritual abuse is that the abuse is perpetrated on the basis of programming. Consequently, the results describing the way in which the various forms of abuse are perpetrated must be interpreted as the means used to facilitate programming. According to the results obtained, programming is a method of extreme psychological abuse created from long series of conditioning. Let's look at the different methods used for programming as presented in the course of this research:

- The provocation of a dissociative state
- Repeating messages
- The use of: simulations; staging; rituals; spiritual or religious symbols; animals; electric shocks; drugs; deprivation.

Induced dissociation

According to some of the results obtained in the course of this research, ritual abusers know about, use and deliberately provoke dissociation in the people they abuse. As one participant put it: *"In order to survive severe abuse, children dissociate and ritual abusers take advantage of this. They will intentionally create dissociation in order to hide what they are doing for a long period of time"*.

A second participant said that extreme dissociation, or multiplicity, allows abusers to programme oblivion or denial of the abuse they commit.

It should be remembered that most of the participants believed that the ability of young victims to dissociate is an important factor in enabling offenders to gain control over their victims. In this sense, the findings on the use of dissociation to facilitate programming are consistent with Gould and Cozolino's (1992) analysis of the importance of victims' age when abuse begins.

"Programmers recommend that mind control should begin before the child reaches the age of six; early childhood is conducive to dissociative states. Drugs, pain, sexual assault, terror and other forms of psychological violence cause children to dissociate in the face of intolerable traumatic experiences. The part of the child that has split in order to deal with the trauma will become extremely porous to suggestions and programming during the abuse". (quoted by Beardsley, 2002, p. 13)

Thus, the results concerning the provocation of dissociation as a method of facilitating programming validate those demonstrating the importance of this impact in ritual abuse survivors.

Using a belief system

As we have seen in the theoretical framework, the presence of a belief system in ritual abuse is one of the first characteristics that made it possible to recognise this type of abuse. In fact, it was at the origin of the first conceptualisation of ritual abuse as satanic abuse. Analysis of the results shows that the presence of a ritual abuse belief system is one of the methods used for programming. In this sense, our analysis differs from the first conceptualisations of ritual abuse. It should be noted, however, that we have recognised various problems relating to the conceptualisation of ritual abuse that arise from the results linked to the use of a belief system.

By comparing the results relating to the presence of a ritual abuse belief system with those describing the methods used for programming, we come to recognise that this is one of the methods used to program victims.

As one of the participants pointed out, abusers use a belief system as a strategy to hide the reality of the abuse they are committing. She said that the beliefs used in ritual abuse are essentially used to terrorise the young children who are the victims. This is the case, she said, with the use of Satanic beliefs.

In the same vein, some of the comments made by other participants also raise the link between the use of a belief and programming.

There may be specific beliefs programmed in. I know that for some survivors there is a religious or spiritual belief used but so far, for the one I'm talking about, we've never been able to identify that they were trying to impose a specific belief apart from imposing terror; really terrorising her and making her powerless.

It should be remembered that more than half the participants said that it was sometimes difficult to associate a religious or spiritual belief with the abuse. In the light of the results obtained, we can say that the groups of individuals who commit ritual abuse mostly use an evil belief or any form of ideology attributing some kind of power to them.

Let us recall some of the beliefs used in ritual abuse mentioned in the course of this research: Satanism, voodoo, Santeria, evil beliefs and more mystical beliefs associated with higher forces or witchcraft. Two participants stated that all forms of ideology and belief are used as justification or backdrop for ritual abuse. In this sense, the use of a belief system essentially makes it possible to terrorise and dominate the victims, which is consistent with the aim of the programming. As a result, the belief is of little importance: it only serves to consolidate the power of the abusers.

As some of the participants testified, there may also be cases of abuse organised around the ideology of the superiority of the white race, as with the Nazis or the Klu-Klux-Klan, or simply the belief that one was born to serve and obey one's father.

It should be noted that only three participants mentioned Satanism in the course of this research. However, two of them felt that Satanism was merely a front for abuse. In fact, one of the characteristics of ritual abuse is that the abusers use a belief to orchestrate their abuse. In this sense, we agree with the participant who said that people tend to pay too much attention to the notion of beliefs and especially Satanism when they talk about ritual abuse. However, there are satanic practices and symbols associated with some of the accounts of ritual abuse. The participants were able to show how the use of Satanic beliefs sometimes manifests itself in ritual abuse. Social workers need to understand that satanic elements are often present in the accounts of ritual abuse survivors, including the practice of satanic rituals and ceremonies.

One of the participants claims that abusers have gambled rightly by using Satanic belief in the context of abuse: attention is diverted from the criminal acts they commit. Instead, people are either attracted by the mysterious phenomenon of Satanism, or perplexed and frightened by what it represents. Moreover, the testimony of survivors who present elements associated with Satanism is often called into question because of the bizarre and implausible nature of their accounts.

Repeating messages

The results show that one of the techniques used for programming is message repetition. According to the results obtained, there are three objectives for this method:

- attributing or implanting a negative sense of identity

- keep victims feeling terrified and threatened

- ensure the silence surrounding abuse

- dictate how victims should behave.

The repetition of negative messages thus aims to transform the victims' sense of identity and freedom. These results correspond to the three objectives of programming according to Hassan (2000, cited by Borelli, 2006). This author says that thought control aims to influence the way a person thinks, reacts and feels.

The use of simulations and staging

This research shows that most of the practitioners interviewed acknowledge that simulations and staging are methods used to orchestrate ritual abuse.

According to the participants, simulations and staged scenes allow abusers to manipulate their victims. As mentioned earlier in this discussion, rituals, i.e. scenarios and staging, can be linked to practices associated with sadism. These methods are essentially aimed at terrorising and confusing victims and making them believe that they have absolute power. Abusers alter reality by changing the context in which the abuse takes place. Moreover, like Sullivan (1989), we believe that abusers also use these simulations and theatrics to protect themselves against all forms of possible reprisal: *the ritual element (e.g. devil worship, animal or human sacrifice) is considered by many to be unbelievable, which undermines the victim's credibility and reduces the chances of obtaining justice for these crimes.* (quoted by Borelli, 2006, p. 27). Creating situations that often seem implausible once again serves to conceal the criminal activities they commit. In connection with the results relating to the different belief systems used in ritual abuse, it is important to emphasise that simulations and staging are not limited to practices associated with Satanism. Here are the related results:

- The staging of spiritual or religious rituals
- The use of spiritual or religious symbols
- The use of ceremonial vestments, including black hooded cassocks
- The use of costumes and disguises
- Simulating a coffin
- The simulation of mystical or supernatural forces
- Murder simulation
- Simulated surgery

One of the participants mentioned that one of the women she accompanied had confided in her that she had undergone an operation as part of the abuse. This participant described this type of physical abuse as medical abuse. This result corresponds to what Sullivan, for the Los Angeles County Commission for Women Ritual Abuse Task Force (1989/2005), calls "*magic surgery*". The presence of blood seems to show the victim that she has undergone an operation. However, this is a method used for programming. This technique essentially tends to silence victims by terrorising them and programming them with the idea that they will be able to find out if they dare to talk about the abuse. The abusers will make the victims believe that they have inserted something into their bodies: a bomb that will go off if they talk about the abuse, or the devil, or the heart of Satan, that will attack them if they do.

As this research has shown, different techniques are used to alter the mental and physical state of victims during abuse. Here's what one of the participants had to say on the subject:

Their mental state has been altered either by the use of drugs or by putting them into a trance state, or by playing music at an extremely high volume, using candles or herbs, abusing the child to the point where he or she no longer has any strength and is completely exhausted. Then they use costumes, lighting and smoke to confuse the person even more. Do I really see a woman being killed? They don't know what's real any more. Everything has been altered. They no longer know what is true in the world because they will sometimes experience or witness things that are not part of reality. It is the change in their mental state that leads them to believe that what is happening is real.

These results show that different techniques are used to create confusion about the reality of the abuse suffered.

As pointed out by Rudikoff (1996), recognition of the use of simulations and staging should in no way minimise the nature of the abuse suffered by victims of ritual abuse. It should be remembered that such abuse is committed against young children and that the resulting trauma is the same whether or not it is staged.

It should be noted that one of the participants presented a more detailed analysis of the reasons why victims are abused at a young age and on an ongoing basis. According to her analysis, the methods of abuse used are linked to the stages of childhood development. However, what she says in this regard seems to corroborate the information shared by other participants. She talks about the different stages associated with training children:

"The emphasis before the age of five is to get the child to be completely destabilised, unable to cope with the abuse and believing that it's her fault. At the same time, it's to get her to be able to dissociate, to "switch"; to have another part of herself that she presents in public and that appears completely normal. They will do this separation continuously in order to manipulate the child into being what the cult wants her to be to meet their needs."

According to this participant, the training becomes more specific after the age of five; it is more focused on abusing others and playing the particular role envisaged by the group. The abusers force the children to abuse each other; in this way, they make them believe that they themselves have done harm. The child is trained in a very specific way to believe that she is responsible for everything that happens around her so that she never reveals anything to anyone. A child is more able to tell if someone else has done something wrong than to admit that she herself has done something wrong. This participant said that during this period, the child must maintain her ability to achieve a state of dissociation in order to hide what is happening at home or during group abuse.

Almost all of the participants (7/8) said that forcing victims to witness or take part in horrible things, including abuse, was one of the methods used in ritual abuse. They described several examples of this in the testimonies of ritual abuse survivors. The survivors told them that they were forced to watch other children or other women being physically and sexually abused. Survivors of ritual abuse were forced to witness horrific things: the murder of babies or people who tried to resist or speak out about the abuse, rape, torture and the birth of babies to be used by the abusers; this sometimes happened during ceremonies.

Appendix 5

Karen Mulder case

They tried to turn me into a prostitute; it was so easy, I couldn't remember anything, I forgot everything... I was a toy that everyone wanted to have.

In October 2001, the famous Dutch model Karen Mulder made shocking revelations during the recording of a television programme. She denounced her alleged sexual exploitation by her family, her entourage and certain high-profile personalities. She said that she had been raped by her father from the age of two, and that she had become aware of this a few months earlier, her memories resurfacing in flashbacks. She also revealed that she was regularly raped by her employers (a famous modelling agency), by people close to her and by members of the Gotha (royal families). She said that she had forgotten her abuse because of hypnosis, or what she thought was hypnosis...

Shortly after these revelations during the recording of a television programme with Thierry Ardisson, she gave an interview to *VSD* magazine, a feature entitled "*Le cri de détresse d'un grand top model*" ("*The cry of distress from a top model*") published in January 2002 in *VSD* N°1271. The magazine revealed that Karen Mulder had been received by the head of the brigade de répression du proxénétisme and that she had told him about dinners organised between young supermodels and *wealthy old men*. The interview gives a number of clues suggesting that she has been subjected to trauma-based mind control. Here are some extracts from the interview:

*Someone in my family (she mentions a name) sexually abused me when I was two. He was a psychopath. He put me under hypnosis. Since then, anyone with authority who knows my secret can manipulate me. **Until I got rid of the terror of my childhood,*** *anyone who frightened me could have a hold on me (...) They tried to turn me into a prostitute: it was so easy, I couldn't remember anything, I forgot everything (...) I was a toy that everyone wanted to have. Everyone took advantage of me (...) I had no will of my own, so they organised my life for me: everything, everything, everything (...) They did hypnotic things to me (...) Yes, it's huge. There's been a whole conspiracy around me for a long time, involving people in the government and the police.*

Everything in my life has been organised! Everything, everything, everything! I had no will of my own (...) During the 'Restos du Coeur', an artist told me: "Someone close to you abused you, they're organising for you to be raped again and for you not to know anything". A famous singer said to me: "Someone close to you (she named a name) told me that you were raped, can you forget about it? Look at me, you'll forget it! And she laughed. And it worked: I forgot (...) I really began to suffer, and that's when I had my first flashes. First of all of someone close to me raping me. I said to myself: that's it, I've found out why I felt so bad (...) In fact, all the people in my family are paedophiles. It's a vicious circle, and today I'm breaking it! (...) I was an asset. My image, my kindness, my goodness, served those who wanted to hide things. And now we're dealing with some very, very, very bad people... Those who wanted to speak out are dead today (...) It was a friend of mine in New York who had me raped by the chairman of a big company. One day she called me up and said: "Do you remember what they did to you when you were very little? I said, "Oh yes, oh yes! - Well, X is going to come and see you, he's going to make love to you and you're going to get the biggest contract there is. I didn't want to, but I was like a doll with no will (...) I want justice, that's all! Paedophilia is still such a taboo. It's girls like that who want to be models. So it's easy for thugs to get power over them.

Is this woman under mental control? Is she a *"presidential model"* (a sex slave programmed from childhood, reserved for the upper echelons of society)? What she describes as memory lapses following the rapes, *"I couldn't remember anything"*, could correspond to **a severe dissociative disorder with amnesic walls**. The fact that she told *VSD* magazine that she was raped under hypnosis *from the age of two*, that her family *only associated with paedophiles*, that it *was a vicious circle that she wanted to break*, and that her sexual exploitation seems to have continued throughout her life, strongly suggests that she could have suffered the sad fate of a mind-controlled sex slave, the prisoner of a network exploiting her dissociative disorder. During the taping of the television programme in November 2001, she also mentioned several names linked to the entertainment industry, saying that these people were either aware, or were themselves rapists or victims. She mentioned the name of another well-known French star, saying that she too was subjected to this kind of treatment.

► folle! Et je sais que la vérité sortira. C'est fascinant ce que j'ai vu, personne ne le verra jamais dans sa vie. Les horreurs, les manipulations... Avant j'ai souvent été mal à l'aise, je culpabilisais. J'étais très très mal dans ma peau. Pour la première fois de ma vie, je suis vraiment fière de moi. Je suis un être humain, quelqu'un de bien.
Je n'ai rien sur la conscience et ceux qui ont quelque chose sur la conscience, ils vont payer.
J'étais un atout. Mon image, ma gentillesse, ma bonté, servaient à ceux qui voulaient cacher les choses. Et là, on a affaire à des gens très, très, très mauvais... Ceux qui ont voulu parler sont morts aujourd'hui.
Pendant des années, vous avez fait un métier très dur. Des rumeurs assez terribles courent toujours sur le monde du mannequinat qui a été longtemps le vôtre.
K. M. J'ai même été porte-parole d'Elite, souvent. Je disais que les parents pouvaient tranquillement laisser leurs enfants dans ce milieu. Aujourd'hui, je voudrais rectifier ! Ne faites jamais confiance à quiconque. Ceux qui vous sou-

AVEC ALBERT DE MONACO. Karen Mulder au bras du prince, en mai 2000 à l'occasion d'un dîner au profit d'une cause caritative. Résidente monégasque, Karen était de toutes les festivités de la Principauté.

"J'étais un jouet que tout le monde voulait avoir. Tous ont profité de moi"

Despite filing a complaint and opening a judicial investigation, her family quickly had her committed to a psychiatric hospital shortly after her revelations... She was only released three months later. Was it then necessary to update the mental programming? After a certain age, amnesic walls tend to dissolve, which is why certain memories resurface in the form of flashbacks.

Her family tried to pass the *incident* off as a paranoid delusional attack, but no one could prove that it was really a case of madness and that what she had said was false.

Certains voudraient la faire passer pour folle. Mais la justice, saisie de l'affaire, enquête.

Le 31 octobre, Thierry Ardisson reçoit Karen Mulder à « Tout le monde en parle ». L'ex-top model, qui faisait partie de l'agence Elite, doit lui faire des révélations sulfureuses sur le monde des mannequins. Et quelles révélations ! Sur le plateau, elle cite le nom d'une haute personnalité monégasque qui l'a, dit-elle, violée. Elle affirme ensuite que des hommes politiques et des P-DG de grosses entreprises se font

SOUS LES PROJECTEURS. Le 9 décembre 1996, Karen reçoit chez elle une équipe de télévision. Aujourd'hui, les micros ne se tendent plus vers elle.

Some time after her forced hospitalisation, the supermodel gave an interview to Benjamin Castaldi on the M6 programme "*C'est leur destin*" in September 2002. A interview in which the doubt still hangs over the fact that she really did try to reveal her condition as a slave under mental control, without even knowing herself exactly what she was in for. Here are a few extracts:

Benjamin Castaldi: *If you had to sum up your destiny in a few words, what would you say?*

Karen Mulder: *On the one hand it's a fairy tale, and on the other it's a horror film, a real nightmare. And when it all came back, there were people who tried to stop me talking. They put me in a clinic to stop me talking. I got out with the help of a lawyer, but it was a whole thing... It was quite complicated! (...) The lawyer phoned me directly in my room. She said: "Listen, you don't look at all like a madwoman! I'm coming to get you in the next two hours". I packed my bags and left (...) Once I'd reached my modelling goal, everything was fine on the surface, but deep down I felt that something wasn't right. So I underwent psychoanalysis for five years, and things came back to me that were so serious that I was becoming paranoid in a way (...) I tried to talk, but they didn't want to believe me. There was a certain amount of paranoia, because it's true that when things are this huge, things get a bit out of hand. There's a bit of delirium. But* the *more time goes by, the more I realise that, in fact, it's not at all (...) Have you seen the film 'True Romance'? That's my life in a way. Everything was organised. Everything was manipulated. I was someone who didn't see anything...*

Following an interview about the Didier Schuller affair, actress and singer Marie Laforêt said: "*I don't know what happened to Karen Mulder, it's the same story, she was talking about the same people, except that she was completely cut off... So they made her a little disc to stamp her with. So she knows that if she ever says anything that she didn't want to say at the time, she'll have an even more miserable fate than the one she has at the moment. So it's in her best interests to keep her head down... That's all there is to it... But she tried! She made an attempt and she paid the price. We amused her by having her make a record, a promo... So everyone else is in on it? You can answer that for yourself... Of course!*"

On 16 January 1998, Marie Laforêt gave evidence on the 8 o'clock news on France 2 about **traumatic amnesia**. At the age of 3 she was raped several times by "a neighbour", a memory that was repressed for years before resurfacing in her forties:

"I relived exactly what had happened, the man's name, his costume, the way he did things, everything? It all came back at the same time. I couldn't talk about it for three days and three nights of crying fits... You can't confuse it with anything else, not with a premonition, not with mental confusion... It's not mental confusion, on the contrary, you're being excessively precise."

Appendix 6

Festen

When cinema plays its part in revealing behind the scenes...

In 1998, Danish director Thomas Vinterberg graced the Cannes Film Festival with his film **Festen** (subtitled *"Family Feast"*), which won the Jury Prize. Here is the synopsis of the film:

Helge is celebrating his 60th birthday. To mark the occasion, he invites his whole family to a big house. During the dinner, the eldest son, Christian, is invited to say a few words: some hard-to-hear truths are revealed...

In this production, Thomas Vinterberg deals with the "family secret", in this case paternal incest within a wealthy upper-class family. Christian, the eldest sibling, was repeatedly raped by his father as a child. His sister Linda, also a victim, did not survive the trauma of incest... she committed suicide.

Thomas Vinterberg has taken care to incorporate a number of elements into his screenplay that suggest that he himself is aware of the hidden workings of certain elitist circles.

The first important point to note is that the character Helge, the incestuous father, is an initiated Freemason. One scene shows the *brothers* meeting in a separate room before the birthday feast. Helge then offers to induct his son Michael into his Masonic Lodge. The second important point is Vinterberg's indirect reference to dissociative identity disorder. The survivor Christian is presented as having an "imaginary friend", an inner companion who follows him everywhere and goes by the name of "*Snoot*". This could mean that the son's personality has split in order to survive the multiple sexual assaults of his sire.

The scandal erupts when Christian, or Snoot... speaks up at the feast: "*It turned out to be a lot more dangerous when Dad was taking his bath... I don't know if you remember, but Dad always wanted to take baths... To do that, he would take Linda and me into his study first. He'd lock the door, pull down the blinds, turn on the lights to make it look pretty and then he'd take off his shirt and trousers... and we'd have to do the same. Then he'd make us lie down on the bench and he'd rape us. A few months ago, when my sister died, I realised that Helge was a very clean man, with all those baths he took. I thought it would be nice to share this with my family... It happened in winter, summer, autumn, spring, morning, evening... and I thought, they should know this about my father: Helge is a clean man... and we're all here tonight to celebrate Helge's 60th birthday! Lucky him! I drink to the man who killed my sister! I drink to the murderer!"*

Following these shocking revelations, Christian's mother, preferring to support her husband, takes the floor to defame and ridicule her son in front of the assembled guests. It is here that we learn of the existence of 'Snoot', Christian's alter personality:

*"You've always been a bit special... I'd say creative like no other! It's amazing the stories he told as a child. I often thought to myself as I listened to you speak that you had everything it took to become a talented writer, I assure you Christian. When Christian was little, and there are some here who may not know this, **he had a faithful companion who never left his side. It was Snoot**. But Snoot didn't exist! Yet Snoot and Christian were always together and always agreed on everything! If there was something Snoot didn't like, then Christian didn't like it either. And if that something was you, too bad for you! There was nothing to be done. But, dear Christian, it's very important to be able to distinguish between fiction and reality. I think that's*

always been a problem for you. I understand that you can sometimes get angry with Dad, but these are things you have to sort out between yourselves. Telling stories like you did tonight, no matter how captivating, is perhaps going a bit too far... **You know, Christian, I think Snoot was very close to you today, and I think you upset your father. So I think it would be appropriate for you to stand up now, leaving Snoot where he belongs, and apologise to your father."**

The alter Snoot, whose traumatic memories are intact and accurate, then goes on to reveal his misfortune:

"I'm sorry to bother you again. In '74 you entered the office without knocking, my dear Mum, and you saw your son on all fours and your husband with his trousers down... I apologise! I'm sorry that you saw your son like that... I'm also sorry that your husband told you to get lost and that you left without hesitation. I'm sorry you're such a hypocrite and such a fake, I hope you die!"

Thomas Vinterberg, who clearly has a good grasp of the subject, has incorporated the "blame game" aspect into his script, with the

aim of destroying the victim's word. First of all, the mother tries to cover up for her husband by pointing to her son's disorderly behaviour to undermine his credibility. Then there's a scene in which the father viciously reminds Christian of his chaotic life, painting a psychological portrait of a victim who has been multi-traumatised since childhood:

"I could stand up too and say a few words to them... a few words about you! About you when you were a child, a sickly child who couldn't stand to see children laugh and be happy! Who spoilt everything for them, on purpose! Who would steal their toys and burn them in front of them, mocking them! About the sick, twisted mind you already had! I could tell them all about how Mum and Dad had to go to France to get you out of that clinic where you'd been rotting for months, literally full of drugs! Totally dazed, much to your mother's despair! I could also tell them about your lack of talent with girls and all the beauties that have passed you by, because the man in you has always been infinitely rare Christian. I could also tell them some fascinating things about you and your sister... Is it that she said goodbye to you Christian? Did she? No, nothing... You abandoned your sick sister, you were absent! All that mattered was you and your twisted brain! And now you've taken it upon yourself to drag through the mud an entire family who only ever wanted you to feel good!"

Finally, it should be noted that Helge, the incestuous Freemason father, himself seems totally dissociated and amnesiac about the paedocriminal acts denounced by his son Christian. After an eventful meal, the two men are alone again in a more peaceful scene:

"I don't understand anything any more, my memory must be failing, I'm getting on in years. Those things you mentioned earlier, I don't remember them at all, you've got to help me Christian... Tell me what happened... "

The script does not tell us whether the father pretends to be unaware of the incestuous acts or whether he himself is a victim suffering from dissociative amnesia and reproducing the vicious circle on his descendants...

Dr Jekyll & Mr Hyde?

Already published

OMNIA VERITAS

MK ULTRA
Ritual Abuse and Mind Control
Tools of domination for the nameless religion

For the first time, a book attempts to explore the complex subjects of traumatic ritual abuse and the mind control that results from it...

ALEXANDRE LEBRETON

MK ULTRA
Ritual Abuse and Mind Control
Tools of domination for the nameless religion

How is it possible to mentally program a human being?

OMNIA VERITAS

OMNIA VERITAS LTD PRESENTS:

If there is one book to cut straight to the core of all the upheaval in the world right now, and what we must do to stop it, this is it.

RED PANDEMIC
THE GLOBAL MARXIST CULT
E. Connor

The critical issue in the world today is Marxism and Marxist indoctrination

OMNIA VERITAS

Omnia Veritas Ltd presents:

TINTIN MY FRIEND
by LÉON DEGRELLE

LÉON DEGRELLE
TINTIN MY FRIEND

Imagine the scandal! Degrelle, the "fascist"!

Omnia Veritas Ltd presents:

THE SVALI CHRONICLES
BREAKING FREE FROM MIND CONTROL
TESTIMONY OF AN EX-ILLUMINATI

The Illuminati are a group of people who follow a philosophy known as "illuminism" or "enlightenment".

THE SVALI CHRONICLES

Understanding the programming of the Illuminati sect

Omnia Veritas Ltd presents:

William Guy Carr

PAWNS IN THE GAME

Here is a TRUE story of international intrigue, romance, corruption, shady deals, and political assassinations, as never before told

PAWNS IN THE GAME

The story is sensational and shocking, but it is educational

Omnia Veritas Ltd presents:

William Guy Carr

SATAN, PRINCE OF THIS WORLD

The Luciferian revolt against God's right to exercise supreme authority over the entire universe was transferred to this earth in the Garden of Eden

SATAN, PRINCE OF THIS WORLD

Now it's up to us. We can accept or reject the truth...

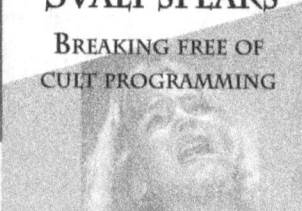

www.ingramcontent.com/pod-product-compliance
Lightning Source LLC
Chambersburg PA
CBHW070903270326
41927CB00011B/2447